York
Hidden Walks

Alan Sharp

Published by Geographers'
A-Z Map Company Limited
An imprint of HarperCollins Publishers
Westerhill Road
Bishopbriggs
Glasgow
G64 2QT

HarperCollinsPublishers
1st Floor, Watermarque Building,
Ringsend Road, Dublin 4, Ireland

www.az.co.uk
a-z.maps@harpercollins.co.uk

1st edition 2022

A catalogue record for this book
is available from the British Library.

ISBN 978-0-00-849633-3

10 9 8 7 6 5 4 3 2 1

Printed in the UK

MIX

Paper from
responsible sources

FSC™ C007454

This book is produced from independently certified
FSC™ paper to ensure responsible forest management.

For more information visit: www.harpercollins.co.uk/green

contents

introduction

York is a city with a rich history. Founded by the Romans in 71 AD as the administrative centre of their northernmost province, it became the capital of the Anglo-Saxon kingdom of Northumbria, and of the Viking Danelaw. Pope Gregory chose it as one of England's two archbishoprics and the centre of the Christian church in the north. From the time of William the Conqueror, many of the kings and queens of England have enjoyed extended stays in the city, earning it the title of The Capital of the North.

Visitors to the city regularly concentrate their stays on York Minster, one of Britain's most magnificent Gothic cathedrals, the quaint haphazard medieval street known as the Shambles, and walks around the old city walls.

But the city has so much more to offer and is small enough to explore very easily. Just a short distance from the city centre you can enjoy beautiful riverside walks, countryside parks, historic great houses and quaint village greens. Even within the city walls there are new things to discover away from the usual tourist trail. From magnificent medieval guildhalls to ramshackle churches, ancient ruins to remnants of the Industrial Revolution, there are surprises around every corner.

The walks in this book are just some of the highlights of this very walkable city and its surrounding villages. Walking in the footsteps of crafty King Richard III, the Victorian philanthropist Joseph Rowntree or the notorious highwayman Dick Turpin, you will discover a side of York you may not have known existed.

about the author

Alan Sharp is a professional tour guide, conducting historical walking tours in York and Edinburgh, and is the proprietor of White Rose York Tours. He has written books and magazine articles on the subjects of history, true crime and mountaineering. He lives in York and has three grown-up children.

how to use this book

Each of the 20 walks in this guide is set out in a similar way. They are all introduced with a brief description, including notes on things you will encounter on your walk, and a photograph of a place of interest you might pass along the way.

On the first page of each walk there is a panel of information outlining the distance of the walk, a guide to the walking time, and a brief description of the path conditions

or the terrain you will encounter. A suggested starting point along with the nearest postcode is shown, although postcodes can cover a large area therefore this is just a rough guide.

The major part of each section is taken up with route maps and detailed point-to-point directions for the walk. The route instructions are prefixed by a number in a circle, and the corresponding location is shown on the map.

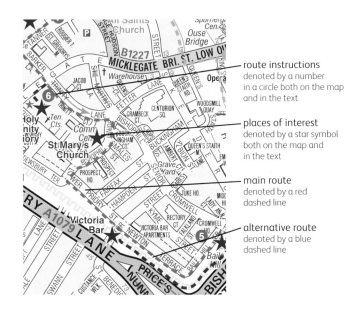

route instructions
denoted by a number in a circle both on the map and in the text

places of interest
denoted by a star symbol both on the map and in the text

main route
denoted by a red dashed line

alternative route
denoted by a blue dashed line

A-Z walk one

Secrets of the City Centre

Hidden gems on well-worn streets.

Even if you have visited the centre of York many times before, there may be things that you have never noticed.

For instance, above the shop doorway on the corner of Minster Gates, is an 1801 painted carved statue of the Roman goddess Minerva, sitting on a pile of books. In Stonegate there is another carving, this time of the devil, dating from the 16th century, although the current one is a more recent replacement. The devil was a medieval symbol of a printer's shop.

In Goodramgate you will see Our Lady's Row. Tourists often pass this row without knowing that they are the oldest remaining secular buildings in the city, built in 1316. Behind them is the Holy Trinity Church, originally built in Norman times, and one of the few remaining churches in Britain with its original medieval box pews. A plaque near the entry gate also tells the visitor that it was the location of the marriage of Anne Lister, better known to television viewers as Gentleman Jack.

Finally the tour visits Museum Gardens where, just inside the gate, you can see some Roman coffins being used as rockery decorations, and shortly after this you pass the York Observatory, dating from 1832. Further into the gardens, the walk passes through the Edible Wood, an often missed gem of a garden in which every plant has an edible element.

start / finish	York Minster West Entrance, Precentor's Court
nearest postcode	YO1 7HH
distance	1¼ miles / 2 km
time	40 minutes
terrain	Surfaced roads and paths, some cobbles.

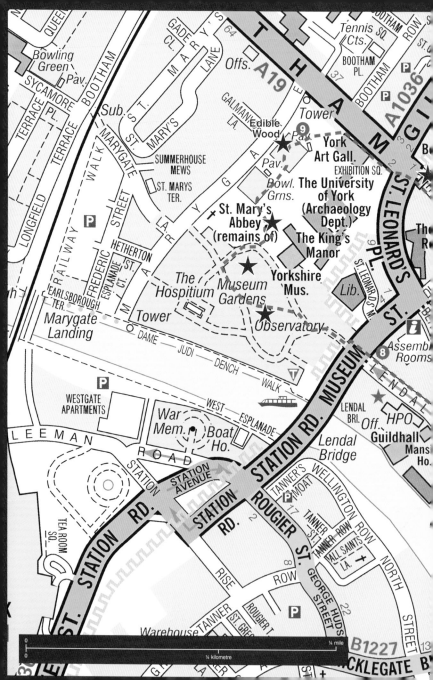

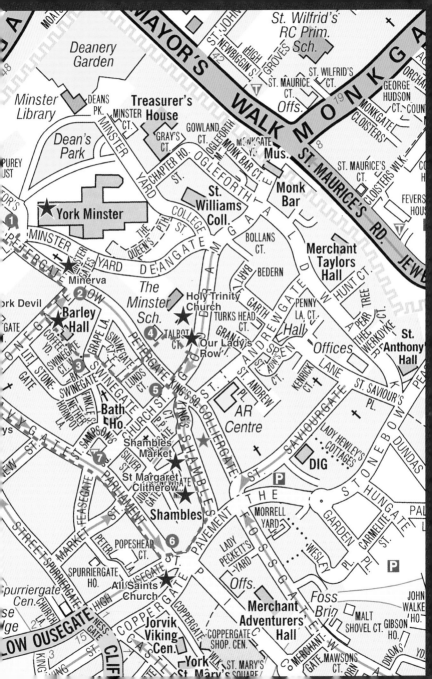

1 The tour begins at the model of the Minster Quarter standing outside the West entrance of York Minster ★ . From here, head across in front of the Minster and keep to the right of St Michael Le Belfrey Church to walk down High Petergate. At the corner with Minster Gates, look up to see the statue of Minerva ★ above the shop door.

2 Take the first turning right into Stonegate, and as you walk along, keep an eye above window level of the buildings on the left. Stop when you arrive at the York Devil ★ , a carved wooden model of a red devil. Underneath this is the entrance to Coffee Yard, one of the city's narrow passageways. Turn left into this passage and follow it to the end.

3 On exiting Coffee Yard, keep going straight ahead along Swinegate, keeping to the left-hand side, and about half way along there is a narrow passage on the left called Lunds Court. Walk through this passage until you reach the shopping street Low Petergate, and directly opposite you will see another passage called Hornpot Lane.

4 If the gate to Hornpot Lane is not closed, then go along this passage and you will find yourself in the churchyard of the Holy Trinity Church ★ . You may want to explore the churchyard, or even go into the church for a visit at this point. Otherwise turn right and follow the path out onto Goodramgate. On the left is Our Lady's Row ★ , and you might want to take a look at these medieval houses before heading to the right up Goodramgate. The Holy Trinity churchyard is not open every day, so if the gate to Hornpot Lane is closed, turn right out of Lunds Court. Then, if you wish to see Our Lady's Row and a view of the church, take the next turning on the left and walk a little way up Goodramgate before retracing your steps back up to the corner again.

5 Turn left into King's Square, and keep to the right-hand side. At the corner turn right and immediately left into the Shambles. About two-thirds of the way down, if it is open, you might want to visit the Shrine of St Margaret Clitherow ★ . You might also want to take one of the passages on the right-hand side and explore the Shambles Market ★ before continuing. Otherwise continue to the bottom of the road and turn right into Pavement.

6 As you walk along you will see the church All Saints, Pavement ★ with its imposing lantern tower ahead of you. Cross the bottom of Parliament Street, which is an open square, and just before you reach the church turn right and follow Parliament Street, keeping to the left-hand side. The middle of this street may be occupied by one of the many festivals or markets that take place here throughout the year.

7 Keep going straight ahead as the road narrows into Davygate, until you reach the corner of St Helen's Square where you will be passing the famous Bettys Café Tea Rooms ★ . Turn left to cross St Helen's Square diagonally, then turn right into Lendal and continue to the end of this road.

8 At the end of Lendal, the gates to the Museum Gardens ★ are directly opposite. Cross the road carefully using the island in the middle, and head into the gardens. Look out for the Roman stone coffins in the flowerbeds to the right. The footpath branches twice here, and you want to take the right branch at the first and the left one at the second, which leads you past York Observatory ★ . Keep going until another footpath turns off to the right and leads to the ruins of St Mary's Abbey ★ . Take this path and follow it through the ruins until it comes out through a large arch at the other side. Then follow it round the gardens where it passes through the Edible Wood ★ into the area behind the York Art Gallery.

9 Veer right across this area and you will find a narrow passage running along to the left of the gallery. Take this and it leads you through to Exhibition Square. Ahead you will see the Bootham Bar ★ , one of the main gates of the medieval walls. Cross the road carefully at the pedestrian crossing here, and then pass under Bootham Bar and go straight along High Petergate until you will find yourself once again in front of the Minster and back at your starting point.

A–Z walk two

Hidden History within the Walls

West of the River Ouse.

On this short walk we explore the side of the River Ouse that is less often visited. The walk starts from The Grand hotel, which was converted from the former headquarters of the North Eastern Railway Company, built in 1906.

The walk passes three important medieval churches which are well worth a visit if they are open. All Saints North Street houses some of the best stained glass windows in the city, mostly dating from the 14th and 15th centuries. St Mary Bishophill Junior has a 10th century tower, much of which was built from stone recycled from the old Roman Colony walls. Meanwhile Holy Trinity in Micklegate was an important Benedictine priory dating to pre-Norman Conquest times.

The tour crosses the river to allow you to see the waterfront warehouses that line the west bank. These have mostly been converted into residential apartments now, but particularly on the Queen's Staith and Bonding Warehouse buildings you can still see the architectural details from their former use, including cranes for unloading cargo.

Other highlights of the tour include Baile Hill, the motte of York's second Norman castle, and Victoria Bar, a gate created in the city wall in 1838 to allow access to new housing developments in Bishophill. The walk ends next to the City of York Council offices, converted from York's first railway station.

start / finish	The Grand (hotel), Station Rise
nearest postcode	YO1 6GD
distance	1½ miles / 2.4 km
time	45 minutes
terrain	Surfaced roads and paths, steps to descend and climb, no steep hills.

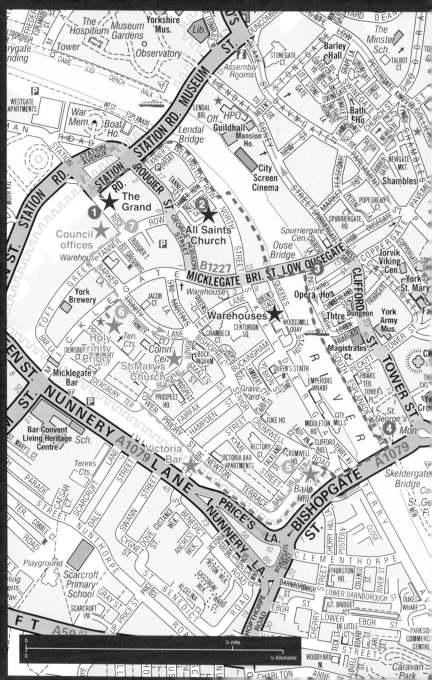

1 Starting from the main door of The Grand hotel ★ , turn right and then right again at the corner of the building. Head directly down this road until you come to the traffic lights then cross at the pedestrian crossing. In front of you, the road heads up onto the Lendal Bridge on the left, but another road to the right, signposted Tanner's Moat, heads down towards the riverside. Take this road and continue down to the corner. Turn right into Wellington Row and walk along as far as the All Saints, North Street churchyard ★ .

2 Note that when the river is flooding, the riverside paths followed to the end of step 4 will be inaccessible. The alternative route is to continue straight along the road from All Saints, North Street and over the crossroads, which will lead you to the turning for Baile Hill Terrace where you can rejoin the route at step 5. When the river is not in flood, cross the road and opposite there is a gate into a small park. Go through this gate and take the path to the left. This leads you onto a concrete walkway which runs along the bank of the river to the rear of the Park Inn hotel. Continue along this walkway until you reach the road again at the Ouse Bridge. Carefully cross the road here and then turn left to cross the Ouse Bridge itself.

3 Immediately as the bridge ends there are some steps down to the riverbank on the right-hand side. Take these and proceed along the riverbank on the King's Staith, noting the warehouses ★ on the opposite bank. A short distance along there is a road that rises away from the river on the left-hand side, ignore this and stay right to continue walking along the riverbank until you reach the Skeldergate Bridge.

4 The walkway continues under the bridge, but to the left there is a set of stairs back up to street level. Take these stairs, and at the top turn immediately back on yourself to cross the bridge. Continue on this road to the next junction on the right. Across from you, you will see the stairs leading up onto the city wall. Turn the corner to find a safe place to cross, then head towards the stairs. Do not take the stairs, but instead turn right to go past them and take the next left into Baile Hill Terrace.

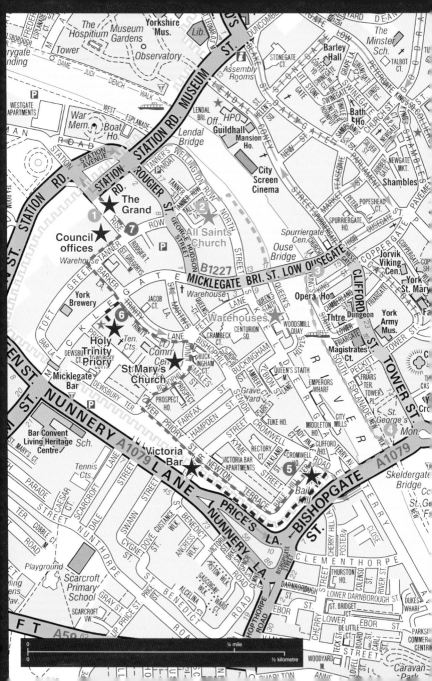

5 For the start of this section, you can choose to walk along the city wall, but if you do, make sure you come back down to the road at the very next set of steps, next to Victoria Bar. Alternatively, continue along Baile Hill Terrace, past the site of the Norman castle ★ , and follow the road round into Newton Terrace. Pass Victoria Bar ★ and continue straight into Lower Priory Street. At the end of this road turn right, and then right again into Bishophill Junior , walking past the church of St Mary ★ . At the bottom of this road is a complicated five-way junction but you want to turn immediately left into Trinity Lane.

6 At the end of this road is the Holy Trinity Priory ★ . If you wish to visit it, turn left onto Micklegate to reach the gate, then after your visit retrace your steps back to this corner. Directly opposite you is a narrow lane leading off Micklegate. Cross the road carefully and walk down this lane until you reach Tanner Row. Cross the road here and turn right to walk beside the fence with City of York Council offices ★ on your left.

7 At the end of the fence is a set of ornate gates with a small pedestrian entrance on either side, which will take you back to the forecourt of The Grand.

A̅Z walk three

Backstreets of the City Centre

The less-seen marvels within the walls.

This walk stays within the city walls, but takes you past some of the tucked-away sites that many visitors miss.

Along the way are two of York's medieval guildhalls, the Merchant Adventurers' Hall and the lesser-known Merchant Taylors' Hall, dating from 1415, hidden away beneath the city wall and now mostly used for weddings and other events. You also pass Rowntree Wharf, a fine example of building from the Industrial Revolution and featuring a nine-storey water tower.

Nearby, you will find a small former Wesleyan chapel where John Wesley himself preached at the opening service in 1759. The tour passes several interesting churches including the medieval St Denys in Walmgate, and the more recent 19th century St George's Catholic Church in whose graveyard rests the notorious outlaw Dick Turpin.

We also pass the Bedern Hall and Bedern Chapel, both dating from the 14th century and respectively the former refectory and private chapel of the Vicars Choral of the Minster.

The walk finishes with a circuit of the Minster. Things of note include the sundial above the door of the south transept, the former private chapel of the Archbishop's palace, and the original statue of St Peter from above the Great East Window, replaced with a newly carved one in 2014.

start / finish	Monk Bar, Monkgate
nearest postcode	YO31 7PD
distance	2½ miles / 4 km
time	1 hour
terrain	Surfaced roads and paths, steps to ascend and descend, no steep hills.

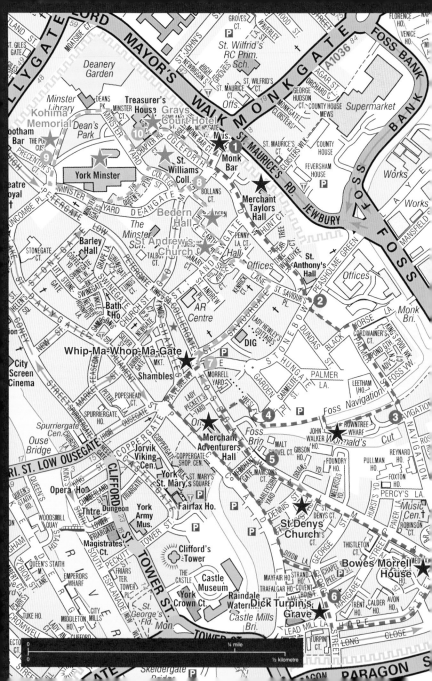

① Starting from the Monk Bar ★, walk in the direction of the city centre and take the first turning on the left, into Aldwark. Pass Merchant Taylors' Hall ★ on your left and continue straight along this road until you reach Peaseholme Green with the medieval Black Swan pub opposite. Cross Peaseholme Green at the raised crossing point and take the footpath signposted for Hungate Bridge between the buildings opposite.

② Follow this path until you reach Black Horse Lane, then turn left and immediately right into Palmer Street, following the sign for Red Tower and City Walls. This path leads you to the modern Hungate Bridge over the Foss. Cross and before the end of the bridge take the set of steps leading down to the right.

③ Almost immediately you will ascend a set of steps up to the timber walkway that runs along the side of Rowntree Wharf, where you will see the converted 19th century flour mill built by Leetham and Sons ★. At the end of this walkway a footbridge takes you back across the Foss and down to street level once again. Follow the pathway along the side of the Foss until it comes to an open area where the path ends. You will see a small gap in the wall with a short set of steps on your right.

④ Ascend these steps and take the short road ahead of you, which is Wesley Place, until you see a small passageway leading to the left between the buildings. Follow this passage and it will take you to Fossgate, one of York's more interesting shopping streets which is often closed to traffic at weekends. Turn left and follow this road across another bridge and keep going straight into Walmgate.

⑤ Follow Walmgate, passing St Denys Church ★ and the unusually shaped medieval timber framed Bowes Morrell House ★. Just after this building, in sight of the Walmgate Bar, turn right into Hope Street and follow this to the end. Turn right, and on the opposite side of the road you will see the graveyard of St George's Church. You might want to take a detour here into the graveyard to see Dick Turpin's Grave which is at the far end and easy to find.

⑥ Return to the road and continue along to Dixon Lane, a small footpath on the left leading you onto Piccadilly. Turn right and then keep straight up Piccadilly, passing the Merchant Adventurers' Hall ★ until you reach the junction with Pavement. Cross Pavement at the pedestrian crossing here, then turn right and continue along past the entrance to the Shambles until you reach an open area signposted Whip-Ma-Whop-Ma-Gate ★. (The meaning of this name is a source of debate, but one theory is that it means 'neither one thing nor the other'.)

7 Turn left then immediately right here into St Saviourgate. Follow this to the end then turn left into Spen Lane. As you walk along you will encounter St Andrew's Church ★ . There is a footpath on the right-hand side which you can take, or turn left then right twice to take you round the outside of the church. Opposite the other end of the footpath is Battle Garth (turn left if you have walked round the church). Walk along here and follow as it turns right to pass the Bedern Hall ★ , then left along Bedern until you come through a covered area back onto the main street of Goodramgate.

8 Turn left then immediately right into College Street, which will take you past the impressive St William's College ★ to the East wall of York Minster ★ . Turn left here and walk through Minster Yard along the South side of the Minster. When you reach the East end of the Minster, turn right to pass the main doors, and through the gate opposite into Dean's Park.

9 Take the left-hand path around the edge of Dean's Park, past the Kohima Memorial ★ which was formerly the archways from a cloister in front of the Archbishop's Palace. Continue past the Minster Library and exit by the gate shortly after, then turn right and pass Minster Court, where through the next gateway you will see the old weatherworn statue of St Peter that used to be above the East Window of the Minster. Continue on past the Treasurer's House.

10 Shortly after you pass through another gate, turn left into Chapter House Street which then turns the corner into Ogleforth. At this corner you might want to detour to look into the courtyard of the Grays Court Hotel ★ . Otherwise, continue along Ogleforth and turning left at the end will return you to Monk Bar.

▲Z walk four

Three Bridges

The River Ouse and Rowntree Park.

For those who only have a short time in York but want to escape the city centre, this is a leisurely walk with plenty to explore along the way. Only the beginning of the walk is on roads, the rest is on public footpaths, away from traffic.

The walk takes in Rowntree Park, created in 1921 and featuring a lake and water cascade, interesting statues, beautiful gardens, and lawns for picnicking. We also cross three bridges. The Skeldergate Bridge is the newest of York's three main road bridges over the River Ouse, being opened in 1881. The Millennium Bridge, which opened in 2001 as part of an orbital cycle route for the city, is for cyclists and pedestrians only. Finally the Blue Bridge crosses the River Foss at its confluence with the Ouse. A wooden bridge was built on this spot in 1738 and painted blue, and the tradition has remained. The current bridge was constructed in 1929 and can be opened to allow boats to pass through.

On the riverside you might notice some tracks from a narrow gauge railway buried in the grass. These were formerly used to supply Fulford Barracks. Further on is the Pikeing Well. The well head dates to 1752 and is a Grade II listed building.

start / finish	Entrance to Tower Gardens, Tower Street
nearest postcode	YO1 9SA
distance	1¾ miles / 3 km
time	45 minutes
terrain	Surfaced roads and footpaths, no steep hills.

1 Start the walk at the entrance to Tower Gardens, which is at the corner of Tower Street and Tower Place, opposite Clifford's Tower. Walk along the pavement heading towards the Skeldergate Bridge ★, and turn the corner onto the bridge itself.

2 Once over the bridge, carefully cross the junction with Skeldergate. Just after this is a pedestrian crossing, and by crossing here you can turn right to climb a sloping pavement with some fencing separating it from the road. At the top of the slope, just past Bishopgate House, there is a footpath leading off to the left.

3 Follow this footpath until it becomes a residential road, Cherry Street, and follow this road until you reach the T junction at the end. Turn left here onto Vine Street, then take the second turning on the right into Lovell Street. A short distance along, a pathway runs diagonally to the left, leading up to a gate into Rowntree Park ★.

4 The quickest route is to follow the path to the lake, then take the path on the left-hand side of the lake and follow it to the other end. At this point, where the path turns back around the end of the lake, there is a curved path off to the left. Follow this path until another path crosses it. Turn left here towards the Millennium Gates, which lead out of the park. If you prefer to spend some time exploring the park, you may take whichever path you wish. From the bridge at the middle of the lake, you could turn left to walk down the Long Borders and explore the gardens on either side, well cared for by the volunteers of the Friends of Rowntree Park. When you have finished in the park, make sure you end up at the Millennium Gates. As you exit through these, you will see the Millennium Bridge ★, a large modern footbridge, on your left.

5 Follow the pathway to the left and cross back over the River Ouse on the Millennium Bridge, watching out for cyclists. When you get to the other side the path splits, so take the one that leads round on the left and joins up to the riverside path. Walk down this path, or if it isn't too muddy then take the dirt path closer to the river. Pass the Pikeing Well ★ to your right, and keep going until you reach a set of gates.

6 Through the gates, turn left and cross the Blue Bridge ★, and at the other side veer right and continue to walk along the riverside. Shortly afterwards you will come back to the Skeldergate Bridge, and this time you will walk through an arch underneath it. At the other side of this arch take the path that goes diagonally to the right through Tower Gardens, and this will bring you back to your starting point.

AZ walk five

River and Road

Floodplains and historical curiosities northwest
of the city centre.

This is a long walk, over six miles (10.2 km), although a shorter version cuts
1½ miles (2.4 km) from the total. It can get muddy so if the weather is wet,
ensure you have good boots. If the river is in flood, the route is impassable.

Beginning at the tourist information centre, the first half of the tour hugs
the bank of the River Ouse, much of it along the embankments that protect
York's northern flood plains. Along the way you can see a variety of wildlife,
mainly jackdaws, mallards and graylag geese, although if you are lucky, you
may spot a kingfisher.

Returning to the city via the main road, you will pass a succession of historic
sites and interesting buildings. The first of these is Clifton Green with its
covered 19th century horse trough, followed by the Burton Stone, whose
bowl was filled with vinegar during plague times to disinfect coins used by
the sufferers.

Look out for St Peter's School, an independent boarding and day school and
the third oldest operating school in the world, founded in 627AD. You will also
pass the Ingram House almshouses, some of the oldest residential houses
in the city dating from 1632. Further down you can see Bootham Park, the
city's former psychiatric hospital. The road ends at the Bootham Bar, the
main medieval city gate on the road to Scotland.

start / finish	Visit York Information Centre, Museum Street
nearest postcode	YO1 7DT
distance	6¼ miles / 10.2 km (4¾ miles / 7.6 km with shortcut)
time	2 hours 30 minutes (2 hours with shortcut)
terrain	Surfaced roads and footpaths, uneven embankment footpath, no steep hills.

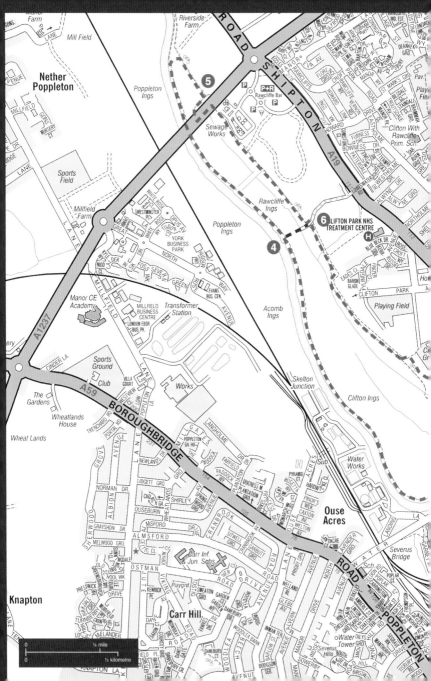

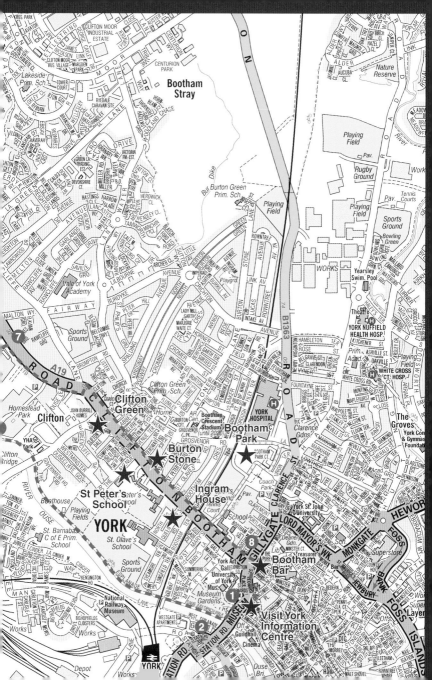

1 Starting at the entrance of the Visit York Information Centre ★ on Museum Street, cross at the pedestrian crossing to the corner of St Leonard's Crescent and Museum Street, then turn left along Museum Street until you reach the gates of the Museum Gardens. Here the road continues across the Lendal Bridge, but to the right of this is another road sloping downwards. Go to the bottom of this road and turn right onto Dame Judi Dench Walk.

2 You are now walking along the side of the River Ouse. Follow this path alongside Museum Gardens and then keep straight to reach the Scarborough Bridge. Go through the foot tunnel of this rail bridge and keep following the riverside path. Continue while it passes under the modern road bridge and until you reach a set of gates.

3 Go through these gates and in front of you is the embankment of Clifford's Ings flood defences. There is a steep path mounting the embankment straight ahead, or if you would prefer a more gradual ascent take the path to the right and then turn immediately back on yourself at the top of the slope. Now cross the sluice gate and walk along the top of the embankment following the river.

4 After about a mile and a half (2.4 km), there is a gate to go through. If you wish to take the shorter route, turn right immediately past this gate, and head towards another metal gate on that side. Go through there and you will join the return route at step 6. Otherwise, if you are following the full walk, keep going straight ahead. The path passes under the York outer ring road and shortly afterwards crosses another sluice gate. Just past this it joins another path in a T junction. Turn right and take the path heading back towards the city.

5 Just before you get back to the ring road there is a gate. Go though, turn right, and follow the path round under the ring road and back the other side. Just before the path rises to join the road, there is another gate on the right. Go through this and follow the path again. Keep following the path through three further gates. After the third gate you will see another path leading off to the left up a slight slope.

6 There is also a dirt path joining from the right. This is where those taking the shorter route will rejoin. Take the left-hand path, and at the top of the slope turn right to walk along the top of the embankment. Keep following this path until you reach the gate to the York Sports Club. Follow the road through the Sports Club as it winds around the rugby pitch. This is private property, and the road is the only public right of way so do not take any short cuts.

7 When you reach the car park of the Sports Club, go out to the road and turn right. You will now follow this road all the way back to the city centre. Keep on the right-hand pavement until you reach the junction with Rawcliffe Lane, then use the pedestrian crossings to switch to the left side and continue along the same road. Cross Water Lane at the pedestrian crossing and be careful crossing all subsequent roads leading off to the left. There are a number of historic sites and buildings to look out for as you head back towards the city centre. Some of these are marked on the map ★.

8 When you reach the city centre again, cross Gillygate at the pedestrian crossing, then just before you arrive at Bootham Bar ★, turn right and proceed around St Leonard's Crescent. At the end you will have returned to the Visit York Information Centre.

AZ walk six

From City Centre to Model Village

New Earswick and the River Foss.

The main objective of this walk is the New Earswick Folk Hall, built in 1907 at the heart of a model community created by Joseph Rowntree to provide the workers at the nearby Rowntree's Factory with affordable housing.

The tour commences at the Monk Bar, the tallest of the four main city gates, the top storey of which was added in 1484 on the instructions of King Richard III. In the same area of the city, the tour passes two rather splendid Victorian buildings, the main building of York St John University, built in 1845, and the old County Hospital building from about five years later.

Much of the tour, though, takes you along paths well known to local dogwalkers but seldom visited by tourists. These take you through marshland, along the riverbank and through woodland, and depending on the time of year there is generally plenty of wildlife and interesting greenery to be found.

start / finish	Monk Bar, Monkgate
nearest postcode	YO31 7PD
distance	5 miles / 8 km
time	2 hours
terrain	Surfaced roads and dirt paths, muddy in bad weather. Some steps.

Folk Hall Café open
Entrance at rear

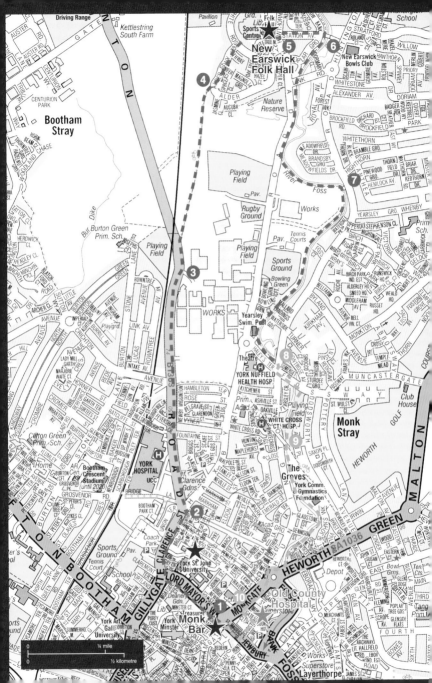

① The tour begins at the Monk Bar ★, and heads in the direction out of the city. At the corner turn slightly left and cross at the pedestrian crossing, then go left again to head along Lord Mayor's Walk. Pass the main buildings of York St John University ★, then turn right onto Clarence Street.

② Continue until the road forks in a complicated junction at a set of traffic lights. Here you need to cross onto the island in the centre of the road, then take the right-hand crossing and head into the road that forks to the left, which is Wigginton Road. Keep going along this road as it leads you out of the built-up areas of the city.

③ You will pass new housing developments and then the entrance to the Nestle factory, and at this point you will see that the pavement ends and a footpath leads away from the road slightly to the right. Follow this path as it passes through a gate, and continue along it until it passes through two more gates and then turns to the right. Shortly after this the path ends in a housing estate.

④ Turn left out of the end of the path and walk along the pavement until you reach a T junction, with a small car park and footpath directly opposite. Take this footpath, which leads into the car park of the New Earswick Folk Hall ★. Keep going straight until you reach the road. If you want to break up the walk, the Folk Hall has a nice café.

⑤ Otherwise, cross the road carefully and turn left and immediately right onto the road that leads perpendicular to the front of the Folk Hall. This is Station Avenue. Follow it until it ends at a small bridge, and just before the bridge take the footpath that leads to the right, along the bank of the River Foss.

⑥ Keep following this path as it follows the river, until it leads you back out onto a main road. Follow this road in the same direction, you will see the river at various points through the fence on your left. As the river veers away from the road, there is a small gap in the fence with some steps, with a finger signpost marked 'Public Footpath'. Head through this gap and resume following the path along the side of the river. As a warning, in winter this part of the walk can be very muddy so ensure you have the proper footwear.

⑦ Shortly afterwards, there is a small bridge across the river on the left. If the river is high, it might be a good idea to cross this and turn right onto the main road at this point, as the river bank further along drops lower and can get flooded. If so, keep going until you reach the next bridge over the river, where you will meet the route again. Otherwise, keep going along the river bank until you reach that bridge, where the path turns right and takes you up some stairs back to the road.

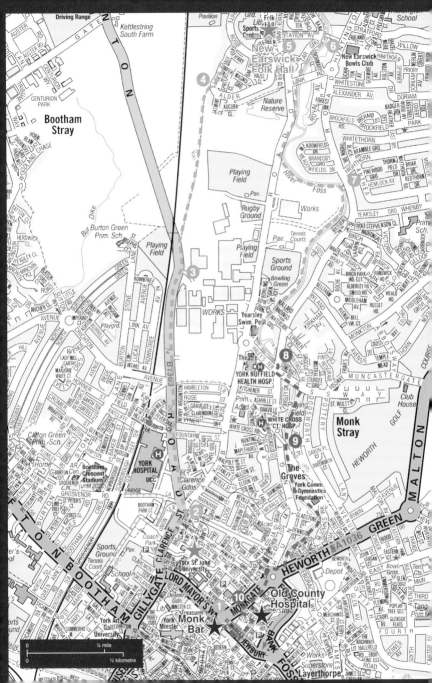

8 Turn right onto the road, down to the crossroads, and use the pedestrian crossings to cross diagonally and take the road leading off to the left and slightly uphill (Fossway). A short distance along there is a gate featuring carvings and labelled 'King George's Field'. Take the set of steps down into a park and walk along the edge on the right-hand side. You will pass three park benches and then see a path leading away to the right. Take this path and it leads you down to the river bank again, but now on the left bank.

9 Follow this path along. It splits occasionally, but as long as you keep following the river bank you can't go far wrong. Eventually, the path rises back up to a gate onto the main road. Turn right as you exit this gate and walk down to the roundabout. When you reach this, turn right and then immediately cross the road using the traffic island, then turn left at the other side.

10 Follow this road going straight and you will see your start point at the Monk Bar ahead of you. If you are tiring at this point you can head straight there, however, if you cross the road at the next pedestrian crossing, you can turn left into Monkgate Cloisters, and this will take you to the old County Hospital building ★. Turn right and follow a path that leads you back to the main road. Turn right, and head along to the end of this road and cross the pedestrian crossing to your left. You will be able to see the Monk Bar just around the corner from here.

AZ walk seven

Pioneers and Survivors

Medieval buildings, Victorian barracks and
a revolutionary hospital.

This walk begins at the Walmgate Bar, the only one of the four main city
gates to retain its barbican. Built during the reign of Edward I, it was badly
damaged during the siege of York, when parliamentarian batteries of
cannon were fired from nearby Lamel Hill. Just outside the bar we will also
see the old 11th century tower of the Church of St Lawrence, the rest of
which was similarly destroyed by the cannons. The new church, built in the
late 19th century, is the largest in York other than the Minster.

The walk also takes you through the Imphal Barracks, York's main army
base named after one of the major Second World War victories against the
Japanese, at which the West Yorkshire Regiment gained battle honours.
There have been barracks in the location since 1795. Behind the barracks is
the Walmgate Stray, a large stretch of land where, in medieval times, any
freemen of the city had the right to graze their cattle.

We also take a circuit around The Retreat. Founded in 1796 by William
Tuke, from a prominent local Quaker family, this facility revolutionized the
treatment of mental illness, pioneering such ideas as occupational therapy
and healthy exercise rather than the chains and manacles in common use.
Widely derided at the time, it later became a model after which asylums
across the world were developed.

start / finish	Walmgate Bar, Walmgate
nearest postcode	YO1 9UD
distance	2¾ miles / 4.3 km
time	1 hour
terrain	Surfaced roads and paths, one moderate hill.

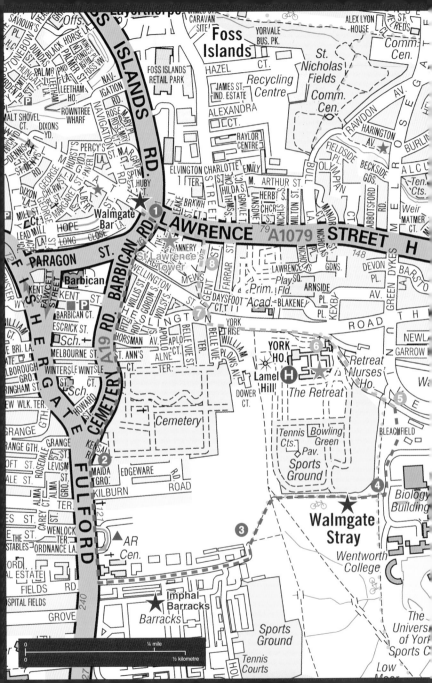

1 Starting from Walmgate Bar ★, head away from the city centre and cross the road at the pedestrian crossing, turning right at the other side. Walk along a short distance to where the A19 forks away to the left-hand side and follow this road. After a crossroads with traffic lights, you will pass York Cemetery on your left-hand side.

2 Shortly after, this road joins the main Fulford Road. Stay on the left-hand side to continue down this road until you find yourself outside the Imphal Barracks ★. Shortly afterwards there is a cycle and footpath leading through the barracks on the left. On the corner is the entrance to the Army Reserve Centre. Follow this path until the end where it turns sharply left and then passes through a metal gate onto the Walmgate Stray ★.

3 A footpath now leads diagonally to the right across the corner of the Stray, and then shortly turns right again where it is joined by a path coming from the Walmgate allotments. The path then passes a red brick wall on your left. This is the rear wall of The Retreat, and behind it is York's Quaker cemetery where many prominent local men are buried including the industrialist and humanitarian Joseph Rowntree. Towards the end of the wall is a plaque indicating this.

4 Shortly after the wall ends, you will pass through another metal gate into the grounds of the University of York. At the other side of this gate turn left, following the signpost for Osbaldwick and Tang Hall. This leads you on a footpath sloping gently upwards. Follow this until just before you reach the road, where the path forks. Take the left-hand fork, and this will lead you to the end of a one-lane road with metal barriers at the end.

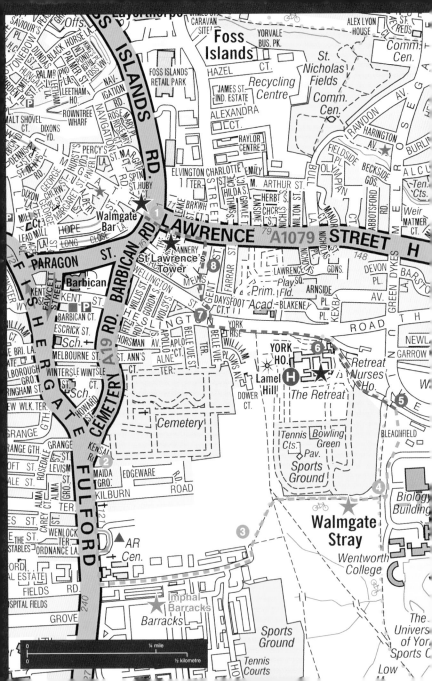

5 Pass through these barriers and follow the road along. There are red brick walls on both sides until it brings you into the grounds of The Retreat ★. Keep following the path going in the same direction, and this will bring you to the main gates of The Retreat, where you can see the main buildings on your left. Pass out through the main gates and turn left along Heslington Road.

6 Once on the main road there will again be a high brick wall on your left, and at the end of this wall there is a small keeper's cottage for the Stray. There are traffic calming measures here so it is a convenient spot to cross to the other pavement. Then continue along Heslington Road as it slopes downwards until you reach the junction with Wellington Street.

7 Turn right here, and in front of you Wellington Street turns away to the left with a junction with Regent Street on the right. Between the two is a footpath leading straight ahead. Follow this footpath as it crosses another road, and you will find yourself walking alongside the churchyard of St Lawrence on your left. There is a gate into the churchyard just as you reach it, and if it is open you might want to go through and head round to the right of the church, passing the tower ★ of the old Norman church on the way.

8 Otherwise, just keep walking down the path until you reach Lawrence Street, and then turn left. Pass the church hall on your left and as you continue along the street you will be able to see the Walmgate Bar and your starting point ahead of you. Continue along the road and cross at the pedestrian crossing to return there. The bar itself contains a nice coffee shop if you feel like some refreshments at the end of your exertions.

Ａ‑Ｚ walk eight

From Gate to Gallows

A history tour southwest of the city centre.

This walk starts from the Micklegate Bar, traditionally considered the most important of the city's four main medieval gates as it stands on the road to London. To this day, when the reigning monarch visits the city they are greeted ceremonially at this gate by the Lord Mayor.

One of the highlights of this walk is the Holgate Windmill. The oldest five-sailed windmill in the country, it was opened in 1770 and has been fully restored to produce stone-ground flour that can be bought here at a Saturday morning market. From here there is an optional detour to the Cold War Bunker which is nearby. In service from the 1960s, this was the regional nerve centre for monitoring fallout in the event of a nuclear war.

The tour also takes in West Bank Park, a small but rather pleasant urban park, and the vast expanse of greenery that is Hob Moor. Said by some to be named after a knight called Hob de Ros, the walk passes the Hob Stone, an inverted grave cover said to bear his image, with a plague stone next to it.

We also visit the site of the Tyburn, York's place of execution from 1379 until 1801. Of the many executions carried out here, the most famous is that of Dick Turpin, the notorious highwayman who became something of a romantic figure through popular literature.

start / finish	Micklegate Bar, Micklegate
nearest postcode	YO1 6JU
distance	3½ miles / 5.6 km
time	1 hour 15 minutes
terrain	Surfaced roads and paths, grassland paths, one steep hill.

SOWERBY

MANOR

SEVERUS

STH.

PATELEY PL.

HEBDON CT.

HEBDON DRIVE

WAITE DR.

HILL CL.

ROAD

BIRSTWITH DR.

BURNSAL DR.

BAILDON CL.

HERITAGE HO.

SHELLEY HO.

★ Bunker

BRAESIDE GDNS.

ELM CL.

HOLGATE LODGE DR.

HOLGATE

CHELWOOD WK.

TISBURY RD.

WK.

ST. SWITHIN'S

Windmill

WINDMILL

RISE

STATION BUS. PK.

BUS. PK. DR.

HOLGATE

HOLGATE PARK

PK.

37

6

②

ROAD HO

ROAD ACOMB

SCHOOL ST.

HOWE ST.

SEVERUS ST.

FAIRFAX CT.

HOBGATE

ROAD

③

106

B1224

④

R O A D

GRANTHAM ST.

WEST BANK

BACKHOUSE

† Holgate

West Bank Park

LANE

MURRAY AV.

LINDLEY ST.

FALCONER ST.

PARK LA.

AVENUE

†

TRENFIE
CT. SPR

Be

LYNDEN WY.

FIRTREE CL.

PARKSIDE CL.

Acomb Prim. Sch.

HOBGATE

KINGSTHORPE

KINGSWOOD DM.

KINGSWOOD GRO.

CARRICK GDS.

NURSERY DR.

JAMES PL.

★

Bowl. Grns.

HILL ST.

NORTHCOTE AV.

BARRETT AV.

BEECH

Our La
Queen of M
RC Prim.

HAMILTON DR. WEST

LADY HAMILTON GDS.

EASTLANDS AV.

STONES CL.

MATTISON

ALLANSON GRO.

HAMILTON

⑤

DRIVE

HAM

ROAD

KINGSWAY

BIRCH COPSE

QUEENSWOOD GROVE

LANE

LINCOLN CT.

ASCOT

ASCOT WY.

WAY

ASHFORD PL.

SANDOWN CL.

WOODFORD PL.

GARTH

ASTON HO.

MERTON CT.

BEVERLEY CT.

HOB

HOBSTON

WINDSOR

NEW-BURY

KEMPTN. CL.

RADFORD HO.

CARLTON HO.

AV.

WEST

Hob Moor Comm. Prim. Acad.

Hob Moor Oaks Acad.

Sports Ground

Club

HAMILTON WY.

CAMPBELL AV.

COLLINGWOOD AV.

HARLOW RD.

HARLOW CL.

CLIVE G

HOLLY

JENNIFE
GRO

HOLLY
BANK

HOLLY GRO.

HOB MOOR

HEATH CL.

HOB MOOR DR.

⑥

★

Hob Moor Gate

Micklegate Stray

WHITE

Hob Moor

GOODWOOD GRO.

Playgrd.

NELSONS

CR.

GRO.

MOOR

0   ¼ mile

0   ½ kilometre

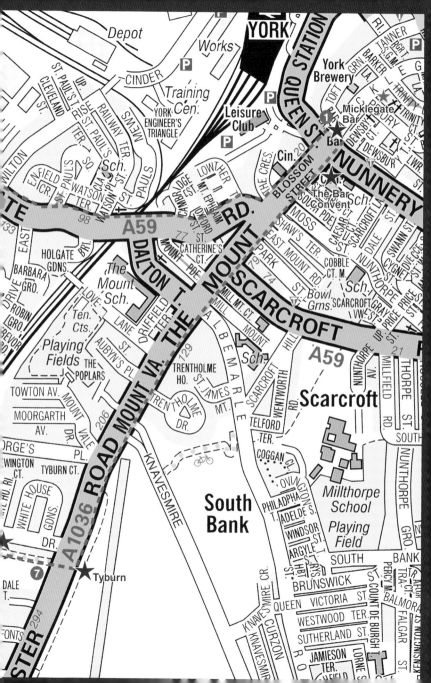

1 Starting from the Micklegate Bar, head away from the city on the right-hand pavement and cross the road at the pedestrian crossing. Go straight ahead along Blossom Street, and keep going until the second turning on the right. Turn into Holgate Road and follow the road, across the railway bridge and continue as the road rises slightly and then drops again. There is a footpath marked on the right, and you can take this to stay away from the main road, or you can continue along the pavement.

2 Either route leads you past the Fox Inn ★ , and just past is a pedestrian crossing leading to a fork in the road. Cross here but keep walking on the right-hand fork. In a short distance the path moves away from the road leading to the corner of Windmill Rise. Turn left here and walk up the steep hill to the Holgate Windmill ★ . Continue until the end of Windmill Rise then turn left into Grantham Drive to reach the main road.

3 If you wish to visit the Cold War Bunker ★ , turn right and take the second right into Monument Close. The bunker is clearly signposted and is at the end of this road. After your visit retrace your steps to the corner of Grantham Drive. Cross the road carefully and turn left. As you walk along, West Bank Park ★ will appear on your right. Continue along the fence until you find the entrance gate at the far side.

4 There are several possible routes through the park to the opposite side. My suggestion is to follow the path round until you see some steps with metal railings on your left. Climb these steps and at the top is a square area with paths going to either side. Opposite is a path with an entrance onto a trellised walkway. Follow the square round on either side to reach this entrance, then go through it and follow the walkway down to where it comes out near two bowling greens. Follow the path round to the left of these, and after the second one a path leading diagonally left takes you down to the park exit.

5 Exiting the park, cross Hamilton Drive to the gates of the York RI Sports Club, then turn left. Take the second turning on the right into Campbell Avenue and walk down to the end of this road. Almost opposite but slightly to the left is a narrow footpath signposted for Millennium Bridge, Foxwood and Woodthorpe. Follow this footpath to the end and you will arrive at the gate to Hob Moor ★ .

6 Going through the gate, take the path directly ahead until you reach a junction with a wooden marker. Here, turn left and follow this path round until you reach another gate. Go through this gate and it will lead you to a tunnel underneath the railway lines. Follow the path through here and onto Little Hob Moor on the other side. Again, keep going straight along, passing the Hob Stone ★ on your left, until you reach the main Tadcaster Road.

7 You will see a pedestrian crossing a short distance away on the left. Cross Tadcaster Road using this crossing. Our route turns to the left, but you might want to briefly explore the area to the right of the crossing which is the site of the Tyburn ★ . The site of the gallows is marked by a stone. After exploring this, return to the main route and continue straight until you return to the Micklegate Bar. Just before you reach it, on your right is The Bar Convent Living Heritage Centre ★ , and you might want to end your tour here with a nice coffee and cake in their refectory.

ᴬƵ walk nine

The Village within the City

Osbaldwick and its beck.

This walk takes you out of the city centre to the picturesque village of Osbaldwick. Once a small village in its own right, it has now been swallowed up by the outskirts of York, but still retains its own unique character. As you walk through the village, on your left is a large village green, while on the right the houses are reached via bridges across Osbaldwick Beck.

Osbaldwick Hall is at the back corner of the village green, and is a Grade II listed building dating from the mid-18th century. The walk also takes you past the 12th century church of St Thomas which, while altered in the years since, still retains some medieval features.

To reach the village we leave the city via the Foss Islands Path, part of the Way of the Roses cycle route, a traffic-free foot and cycle path that cuts through the suburbs of the city. On the return journey we take a walk through Hull Road Park, a 25-acre urban park with the path again following the line of Osbaldwick Beck.

Finally the walk takes you through St Nicholas Fields, a large nature reserve on what used to be grazing land for the monks of St Nicholas' Hospital. While the route of the walk takes you straight through this area, there are plenty of small paths off to the sides of the main route for the more adventurous to explore.

start / finish	Foss Islands Retail Park, James Street
nearest postcode	YO31 7UL
distance	3½ miles / 5.75 km
time	1 hour 30 minutes
terrain	Mostly surfaced roads and paths, one unsurfaced path.

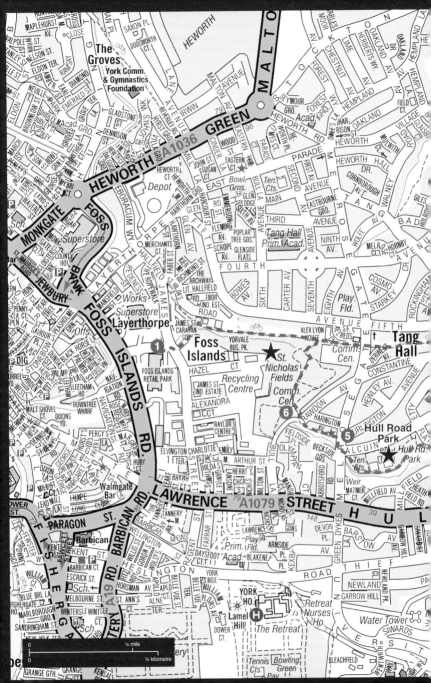

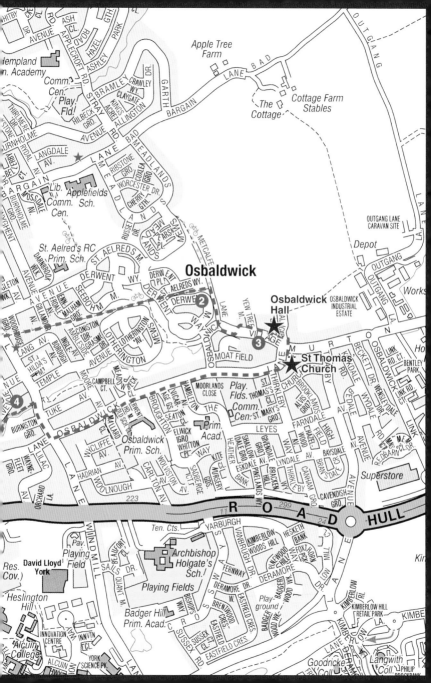

We start the walk at the bus stop in Foss Islands Retail Park, which can be reached on foot from the city centre in about 10 minutes, or by bus. If coming by bus, you will need to cross to the other side on alighting and turn left onto the footpath behind the opposite bus shelter.

1 Follow the path from behind the bus shelter as far as James Street, then use the pedestrian crossing to cross over the road. Here you will find a gap in the fence signposted 'Foss Islands Path'. Pass through this and follow the path as it turns left across a bridge and then immediately right again. Keep following the path for the next 1¼ miles (2 km). Be mindful of bicycles, as this is part of the Way of the Roses cycle path.

2 The path ends in a T junction with a one-track lane. Turn right and follow this along, being careful of any traffic as there is no pavement. At the end of this lane, turn left into the main street of Osbaldwick Village. You will have to cross the road, as there is no pavement on the left-hand side, and then as you reach the village itself you will need to cross again as the pavement on the right ends and one on the left begins. On your left you will pass the Derwent Arms, a lovely 19th century public house which is a perfect place to stop for refreshments.

3 Keep going through the village past Osbaldwick Hall ★ on the left, then turn right at the stone bridge just before St Thomas' Church ★. Follow this road as it curves to the right and heads back towards the city. Continue to follow this road for about half a mile (800 metres) until you reach the crossroads with Tang Hall Lane. Cross carefully, turn right and head along this road until you reach the gates of Hull Road Park ★ on your left.

❹ Follow the path through the park that skirts Osbaldwick Beck, keeping it just on your left-hand side until the last few yards when the path veers away from the stream towards the gate at the opposite corner of the park. Go through this gate and carefully cross the road. Turn right, and then almost immediately left onto a footpath at the head of which is a signboard reading 'Welcome to St Nicholas Fields' ★ .

❺ This footpath is not paved and can be muddy in bad weather. If you would prefer to stick to paved surfaces, keep going until the next turning on the left, and at the end of this road turn left again and, where the road ends, head through a little cutting which will bring you to the end point of the footpath. There is another footpath directly opposite the previous one (or turn right if you used the road route), which leads through some grassland with a children's play area on your right.

❻ When this path joins another paved footpath very shortly, go to the right and follow this new path. This path ends, after a short while, at a T Junction with Foss Islands Walk. Turn left and retrace your steps back to the main road, being sure to take the left fork each time the path divides. At the end of the path you can then re-cross the road back to your start point.

A-Z walk ten

Discovery Trail

Traditional and modern architecture on the
University campuses.

With a student body of around 20,000, the University of York is an integral
part of the city. This walk around the grounds may provide something for
the parents of prospective students to do while their children are having
interviews or campus visits. Or it may be a way for the students themselves
to see the full scope of their new home, or for anyone else who wants a
chance to see the campuses from a different angle.

The main part of the University occupies two campuses and a science park.
These are built around lakes and some nice countryside grasslands. This
walk skirts the East Campus and the Science Park, while walking through
some of the more interesting parts of the West Campus. It takes in the
inclusive rainbow crossing created by students in the colours of the LGBT+
Progress Pride flag.

Further into the campus you pass The Quiet Place, a garden for silent
reflection which has unusually shaped topiary. You will also see Heslington
Hall, a manor house originally built in the 16th century but now housing the
main administrative functions of the University.

start / finish	University of York Campus Central/Market Square
nearest postcode	YO10 5DD
distance	5¼ miles / 8.5 km
time	2 hours
terrain	Mixture of surfaced and dirt paths and roads.

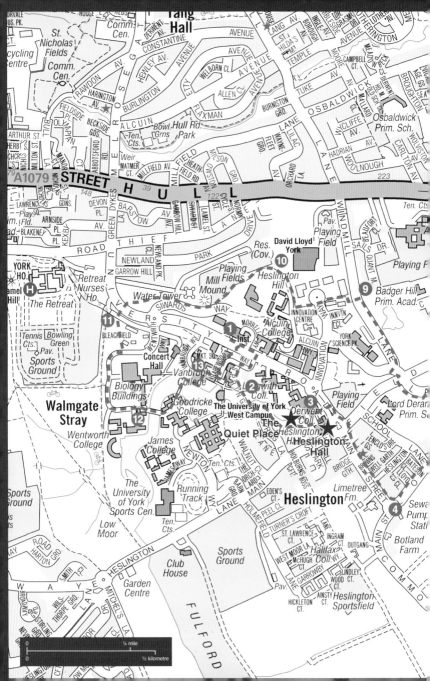

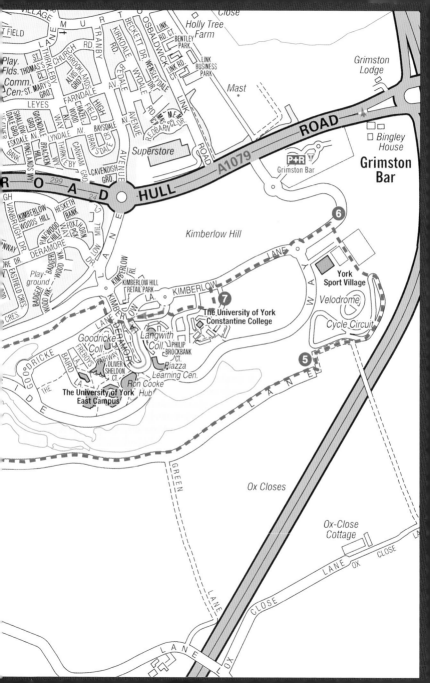

There are a number of bus services running to the university, including buses that stop at the Campus Central stop opposite Market Square. There is also plenty of pay and display visitor parking nearby.

1 From the bus stop, cross the road, turn left and then take the first turning on the right. Follow this road around the car park, crossing at the Progress Pride crossing, and shortly afterwards a public footpath leads away to the left, alongside some buildings.

2 Follow this path until you reach a footbridge over the campus lake, and after crossing this bridge turn immediately left. Follow this path around the edge of the lake, past The Quiet Place ★ and towards the rear of Heslington Hall ★ .

3 As you reach the end of the lake, ahead of you there is a grassy area on the other side of which is a brick wall with a small doorway-sized gap. Go around the grass to either side and pass through this gap and continue to the road. Turn right, and at the junction at the end cross carefully and go straight on. You will now be walking down the picturesque Main Street of Heslington village.

4 At the other end of this street is a mini roundabout. Turn left following a direction marker for Low Lane, and at the end of this road turn right to pass The Crescent. As the houses end, a narrow road continues on; this is Low Lane. Continue along this road, being careful as there is no pavement although the road itself is seldom used by traffic.

5 The road ends with an abrupt left turn onto a gravel road, which then turns right and follows the fence of the York Sport Village. When the path takes a sharp right turn towards a bridge over the York ringroad, there is a narrow dirt footpath ahead of you continuing alongside the fence. Take this path and follow it all the way to its end, where it becomes a surfaced path again leading up through the sports village.

6 When this path reaches the road, cross and turn left and follow the footpath alongside the road. When you reach a roundabout, go straight ahead and the footpath crosses to the left of the road. Along here you will find some interesting signboards giving information about archeological finds made during construction of the East Campus. Shortly after this is a junction on the left, and on crossing this the path turns abruptly left.

7 Keep following this path as it winds through the edge of the campus until it emerges behind a car park. Turn left again and continue to where the road curves right. When you come to the junction of Deramore Lane and Goodricke Lane, cross this latter and follow the surfaced footpath sloping upwards on the other side. Shortly afterwards, turn left onto a dirt footpath and follow it to the end.

8 Where the path emerges onto a brick-surfaced road, turn right and cross where the footpath does. Follow this footpath until it reaches the main road. Cross this road following the signpost for Science Park and on the other side of the road take the turning on the left, and then almost immediately right into Windmill Lane, following the signpost for Hull Road and Tang Hall.

9 Shortly afterwards, turn left at some metal barriers, onto a foot and cycle path signposted for University (West) and the Millennium Bridge. Follow this path as it winds its way into the Science Park, until it crosses a road next to a roundabout. Go straight across and continue to follow the path until it reaches a T junction. At this point, turn right, signposted for Fulford and Millennium Bridge.

10 Follow this path as it curves around a series of buildings, before joining the road and passing through a heavily wooded area. As you emerge from the trees, the footpath branches away from the road again on the right-hand side. Follow it as it goes downhill and through an underpass. The path now crosses another road, and then is joined by a second path from the right.

11 Continue downhill on the path to where it joins a road called Wentworth Way. Continue to follow the road as it turns left in between a car park and some university buildings. Just before this road turns sharply right again, there is a turning on the left with a set of steps after it. Ascend these steps and turn right onto the footpath. This will lead you to a bridge over the University lakes.

12 Cross this bridge, and at the other side turn left onto the road that crosses the path, and this will lead you to a second bridge, over a wider part of the lake. Cross this also, and then turn right and follow the covered walkway alongside the lake. At the next corner turn left and ascend the slight slope then turn right again and pass along the front of the Vanburgh College buildings until you see the Berrick Saul Building ahead of you.

13 Turn left here, you will see an interesting graphic of the University's place in the city on your left. Go straight ahead of you, until this road curves slightly right and emerges next to a car park. Turn left past the car park and it will lead you back to your start point.

▲Z walk eleven

Rawcliffe Ramble

Suburban lake and country park.

Rawcliffe is an affluent area in the very north of York. It is a mixture of recently built and older houses, and is a very pleasant area to take a walk, particularly as most of the walking is away from busy roads.

The main objective of this walk is a circuit of Rawcliffe Lake. Although this is a man-made lake, built to be the focus of the local storm water drainage system, it makes for a pleasant oasis in the middle of this otherwise urban area, attracting a certain amount of wildlife and with grass banks that are perfect for a picnic.

The walk finishes with a cut through one end of Rawcliffe Country Park. Standing next to the Park and Ride, around 2,000 trees and 1,500 woodland shrubs have been planted to develop this area, making it an interesting place to take a wander around after the walk. The park also has a children's playground if you have younger walkers with you.

start / finish	Rawcliffe Bar Park and Ride, Shipton Road, Rawcliffe
nearest postcode	YO30 5XZ
distance	2¾ miles / 4.5 km
time	1 hour
terrain	Mostly surfaced roads and paths, one dirt path and some grassland. One stile.

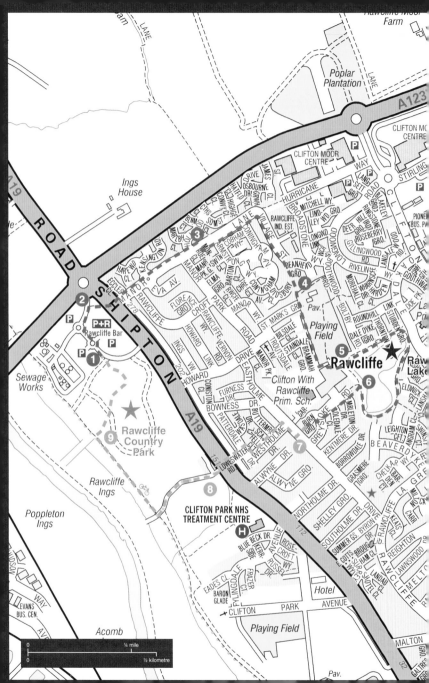

We start from the bus stop at Rawcliffe Bar Park and Ride. This can be reached by the Number 2 Park and Ride bus service, and there is also plenty of parking. Be aware that the car park is locked at 11.05 each evening.

1 From standing in front of the main building, go to the left-hand side and cross the pedestrian crossing, then turn left and follow the footpath round the roundabout and onwards where it turns to the right. Just before you reach the York ring road there is a footpath on the right.

2 Follow this footpath, and at the end of it carefully cross the road. Turn right and immediately left, where you will see a footpath sign slightly removed from the road. Take this path, it follows the line of Manor Lane but for most of its length is separated from it by hedgerows. After a while the path rejoins the road through some metal barriers, at this point turn left to continue along the pavement.

3 Just after the turning to Hollywood Drive you will need to cross onto the other side of Manor Lane as the pavement ends on the side you are on. Continue along until just after a row of trees on your right, there is an open area with a footpath leading to the right. Follow this footpath down through a grass area, ignoring any turnings on your right, until you arrive at a metal barrier with a children's play area behind it.

4 Keep to the right of the play area and the pavilion behind it, and you will see another footpath running down the side of Rawcliffe recreation ground, signposted for Rawcliffe Lake. Take this path to the other end of the recreation ground, where it turns sharply left and then right again over a small wooden bridge. Turn left after the bridge, following the signpost for Lakeside Primary School and Clifton Moor.

5 This path takes you through some metal barriers and then turns diagonally to the right. Shortly afterwards there is a dirt path leading to the left which becomes surfaced again after a few yards. Take this path, or if you prefer to remain on surfaced paths continue a short distance and you will see a turning going back on yourself which will lead you to the same place. This path will take you around the entire perimeter of Rawcliffe Lake ★ .

6 Follow the path around three sides of the lake until you are almost back where you started. You will be able to see a sluice gate ahead of you, and a path leads off to the left next to a lamp-post. Take this path and it leads you to Greystoke Road. Follow this until there is a fork in the road, and take the right fork into Garburn Grove. At the end of this road is a short footpath.

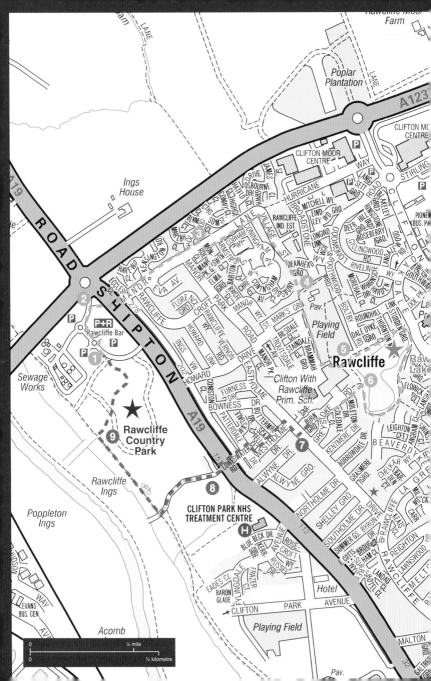

7 At the end of this footpath turn right and immediately left into Westholme Drive. Follow this road until it turns right into Patterdale Drive, then turn almost immediately left into Loweswater Road. At the end of this road you will arrive at the main A19 road, and immediately opposite is the entrance to Shipton Road allotments. Cross carefully and head for the metal gate you can see. There is a pedestrian gate to the right of this gate, go through this and follow the path straight ahead.

8 Shortly afterwards there is another metal gate with a pedestrian gate this time on the left. Go through and continue following the path until it reaches a surfaced path running across it, signposted as cycle route 65. Turn right and follow this path along. It will lead through two metal pedestrian gates, and then just before a third one is a wooden stile on the right.

9 Cross this stile into Rawcliffe Country Park ★. You will be able to see a footpath through the park ahead of you, leading to a large clump of trees. Follow this and pass on the left-hand side of these trees, and you will shortly see a wooden fence containing a children's playground on your left. Follow the fence round, and you will see a wooden gate next to a flagpole. Go through this gate to return to your start point.

A/Z walk twelve

Alms and Arms

Fulford and Germany Beck.

While the Battle of Hastings may be the most well-known battle fought in 1066, two other major battles were fought in the run up to it, both in the York area. In the first of these – the Battle of Gate Fulford – English Earls Edwin and Morcar tried to defend York against the advancing Viking army of Harald Hardrada. The fiercest fighting took place near Germany Beck, in an area we will be visiting on this walk.

Beginning the walk near St Oswald's Church in Fulford, on the southern outskirts of the city, we quickly pass the Sir John Hunt Memorial Homes. Comprising three rows of gabled red brick houses around a square garden, these were provided in the will of brewer John Hunt as almshouses for those who were unable to maintain themselves due to ill health.

We also pass along through Fulford Ings and its riverside moorings. The ings is a wildlife area that gets quite overgrown at times, but the pathway through it is quite well defined, and you will pass an area with a riverside view and wooden tables that makes a great picnic spot.

start / finish	**Opposite** St Oswald's Church, Main Street, Fulford
nearest postcode	YO10 4HJ
distance	2 miles / 3.5 km
time	45 minutes
terrain	Roads with some paved and some uneven pathways.

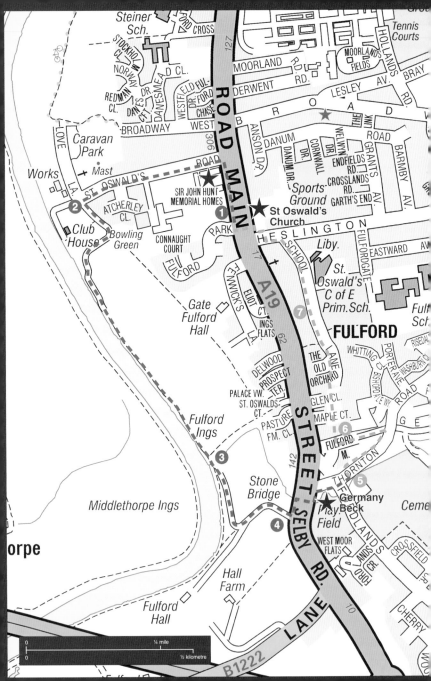

The walk begins opposite St Oswald's Church ★ in Fulford, which can be reached by various bus services from the city centre. By car, there is on-street parking in either St Oswald's Road or Heslington Lane.

1 Facing the church from the bus stop across the road, head to your left, back towards the city centre, and you will very quickly be walking past the Sir John Hunt Memorial Homes ★. Take the first turning on the left after these, which is St Oswald's Road, and walk down until almost the very end of this road.

2 Just after a row of new-build houses there is a crossroads, with a gravel road leading away to the left between two brick walls. On one corner is a sign reading 'Fulford Ings & Moorings'. Turn and follow this road as it turns first right then left and enters the moorings. Continue along, and just after the last of the moorings the gravel road becomes a dirt path. Keep going straight along the riverside for about half a mile (800 metres).

3 Shortly after passing a metal gate you will see some picnic tables on your right. Just past this the path forks, with the right-hand path leading to a gate through a fence. Take the left path, which gradually moves away from the river, and after you see a metal entrance with a finger post next to it, the path turns almost back on itself, following the path signposted 'Millennium Way'. Follow this on round and after passing a metal gate it becomes first a gravel road and then a surfaced one.

4 Shortly afterwards the path starts to ascend with a brick wall on your left and a metal height barrier ahead. This brings you back to the main A19 road. Turn left and then cross at the pedestrian crossing. Go left after the crossing and then turn right into Thornton Road. As you turn the corner, on your right is a medium-height red brick wall on the other side of which is Germany Beck ★.

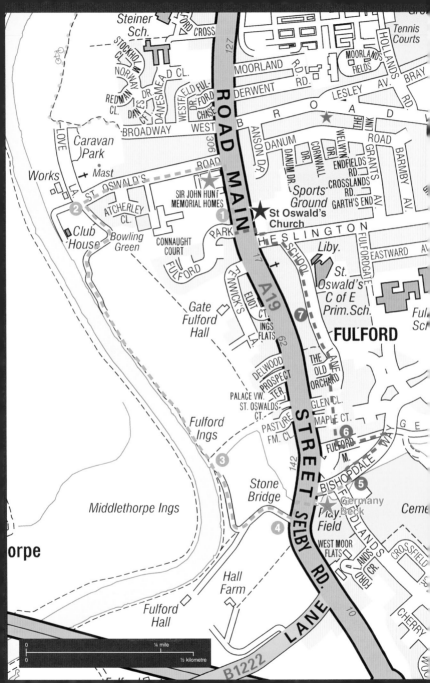

5 Walk along to the corner where the pavement ends just after a turning on the right for Fulford Cemetery. Cross to the other side then continue to follow Thornton Road. The road continues to follow the line of the beck until it curves round to the left, and just before entering a modern housing development there is a gravel footpath on the left. Take this path and follow it along the front of the modern housing.

6 Just before arriving at an older red brick house, there is a surfaced path leading to the right with two metal barriers at the end. Turn onto this path and follow it along as it narrows between a wall and a hedge, and then arrives at another metal barrier. Passing this, you are near the end of a cul-de-sac. Turn right onto the road and follow it along. There is pavement only on the left of the road.

7 Continue down this road as it passes a children's play park and then a school on the right. Once you arrive at a T junction with Heslington Lane, turn left and at the next corner you will be back at the main A19 road. There is a pedestrian crossing ahead of you, and if you cross this and turn right, you will return to your start point.

ᴀᴢ walk thirteen

Bishopthorpe and the Solar System Way

The Archbishop's palace and a path that flies you through space!

The beginning of this walk follows part of the Solar System Way, a scale model of the planets of the solar system that extends over 6½ miles (10.3 km) of the York to Riccall cycle route.

The walk also takes in the village of Bishopthorpe, just outside the ring road to the south of the city, where we pass Bishopthorpe Palace, the traditional home of the Archbishop of York that was originally built as a manor house in 1241. Parts of the palace are visible from the road, albeit behind the 'strawberry gothic' gatehouse constructed in 1765.

A small detour onto the riverside takes you past the ruins of the old St Andrew's Church, dating from the 1760s. The church here was replaced in 1899 on a new site after the river flooded in 1892 and washed bodies out of the graveyard.

An optional addition to this walk is a visit to the popular Askham Bog, an area of peatland that is a Site of Special Scientific Interest and part of the ancient fenlands of Yorkshire. The directions for this addition are on pages 84–85.

start / finish	Askham Bar Park and Ride, Tadcaster Road (A1036)
nearest postcode	YO23 2BB
distance	4 miles / 6.5 km (+ optional 1¾ miles / 3 km)
time	1 hour 45 minutes (+ optional 45 minutes)
terrain	Surfaced roads and paths. Optional extra includes dirt paths, which can be very muddy.

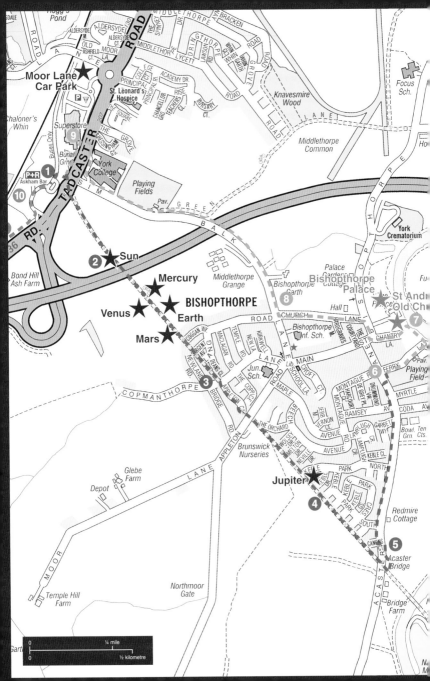

The tour commences from the Askham Bar Park and Ride, which can be reached from the city on the dedicated Park and Ride number 3 or 3A buses. The Park and Ride car park does not permit you to park there and walk, so if you are coming by car, park in the nearby Moor Lane car park ★ and walk the few hundred yards past the supermarket to the Park and Ride bus terminal.

❶ Standing in front of the terminal, take the path that leads down to the road on the left. At the bottom of the path, go through the wooden gate and follow the path to the left, signposted to Bishopthorpe and Selby. This descends in a spiral to an underpass beneath the road, and having passed through, follow the footpath directly ahead.

❷ This path leads to a second underpass, this one under the main A64 road. Just before this underpass you will see the large model of the sun suspended above your head. A fingerpost here directs you again towards Selby, underneath the underpass. Keep following this route, and you will see the models of Mercury, Venus, Earth (and the Moon) and Mars ★ . Shortly after passing the Mars model you will find the path lined by fences and houses.

❸ A short distance after this the path ends in a housing estate. Here you turn left and then immediately right

into Appleton Court. You should see another signpost for Selby and the Trans Pennine Trail. Follow Appleton Court to its other end where, turning left, you will return to the footpath, passing underneath a road bridge. A little further along this path you will pass the model of Jupiter ★ , and find you have houses on the left of the path and open fields on the right.

❹ Shortly after this, a dirt path leads off to the left and runs parallel to the paved path but slightly higher up. You can take this path if you wish, it leads to the same place. Where it ends and rejoins the paved path is just before a bridge over the road, and at the other side there are steps down on the left. Take these steps down to the roadside, or if you prefer you can carry on a short distance where there is a pathway on the left turning back on yourself and leading down to the same spot.

❺ At the roadside, turn right and a short distance along cross the road carefully as there is only a pavement on the left-hand side. You will now be walking along a road with modern houses on your left, and open fields with the occasional old farm cottage on your right. After a while houses start to appear on the right as well. Soon you will come to a row of shops on the left and a large sports field on the right. Cross the road again at this point, and at the end of the sports field turn right into Ferry Lane.

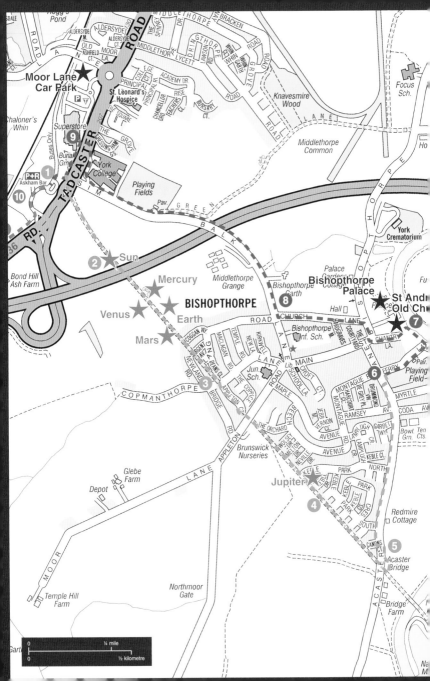

6 Continue to the end of Ferry Lane, taking care as this is a one-track lane with no pavement. At the end of the lane, you are at the Bishopthorpe boatyard. In summer there are often refreshment stands here, if you want to stop and admire the riverside view. Otherwise, turn left along the riverside path. This takes you to the start of the grounds of Bishopthorpe Palace, and then turns left to take you around ruins of the old St Andrew's Church ★ .

7 Go through the gate at the end of this path and walk along Chantry Lane back to the main road. At this point, turn right and you are walking in front of Bishopthorpe Palace ★ . Cross the road where safe to take the next turning on the left, just before the new St Andrew's Church, into Church Lane. Keep going to the end of this road and then turn right onto Sim Balk Lane.

8 This road soon takes you across a bridge over the A64, and a short distance after you will see York College on your right. Just before you reach the corner there is an entrance into York College, and you can take a short cut through here onto the main road, which brings you out next to a pedestrian crossing. Otherwise, go to the corner and turn right, continuing along the road to the pedestrian crossing.

9 Once across, turn left to return to the Park and Ride (or if you parked at Moor Lane car park, turn right). To get to the Park and Ride, walk until the road takes a semi-circular turn on the right, and shortly afterwards there is a gap in the hedge which takes you back through to the bus terminal.

Turn the page for directions for the optional extension of this walk to Askham Bog.

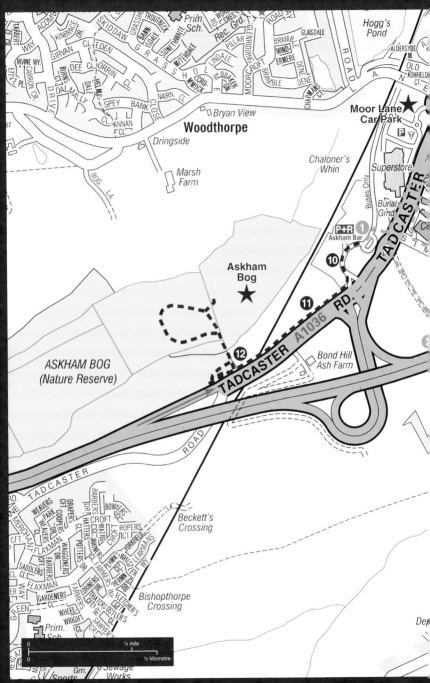

Optional additional walk

10 If you would like to visit Askham Bog, on returning to the Park and Ride, continue past and use the marked footpaths to find your way to the Park and Ride entrance. Keep to the right of the entrance as you leave, and the path turns and runs along the side of the main road. As you continue along you will eventually come to a bridge with a metal covered walkway. Continue across to the other side.

11 The path continues, separated from the road, until you reach a gravel car park. If you came to the walk by car and parked at Moor Lane, you may want to drive along and park here. About half way along the car park on the right, you will see a wooden gate with an information board next to it. This is the entrance to the bog.

12 Go through the gate, and along a dirt path until you encounter wooden boardwalks. These take you in a circuit around the bog. Turn left and follow the boardwalks round. You are allowed to explore the rest of the bog, but it is very muddy so if you wish to do this, it is advisable to have very strong waterproof boots or wellingtons. About three-quarters of the way there is a separate boardwalk off to the right leading to a small pond where some of the most interesting insect life can be found. It is only a short detour and worth seeing. Once you return to the point where you started the boardwalk section, simply retrace your steps back to Askham Bar Park and Ride.

Az walk fourteen
A Countryside Church
Haxby and All Saints Church.

Haxby is mostly a commuter town for York today, although it's origins are as a Viking settlement, and it is mentioned in the Domesday Book. It was a small village in the Forest of Galtres until deforestation, after which it expanded. This walk only passes through the edge of the town, but there are some nice Victorian houses along the way, and just before the level crossing is a rather quaint railway cottage.

Most of the walk is along countryside paths, the first section being alongside the River Foss. As you pass along this path there are a number of small enclosures to explore, one in particular behind a gate labelled 'Woodland Walk and Pond (Deep Water)' is well worth a short detour.

Near the start of the walk, and again towards its end, you will pass the All Saints Church. With a chancel dating from the 15th century, this church stands out in its rural location between the parishes of Huntington and New Earswick. Its picturesque setting makes it very popular for weddings and christenings, and the churchyard is shaded and pleasant.

start / finish	The Blacksmiths Arms, The Old Village, Huntington
nearest postcode	YO32 9RB
distance	3¾ miles / 6 km
time	1 hour 30 minutes
terrain	Mostly pathways of mixed terrain, some paved road. Some stiles.

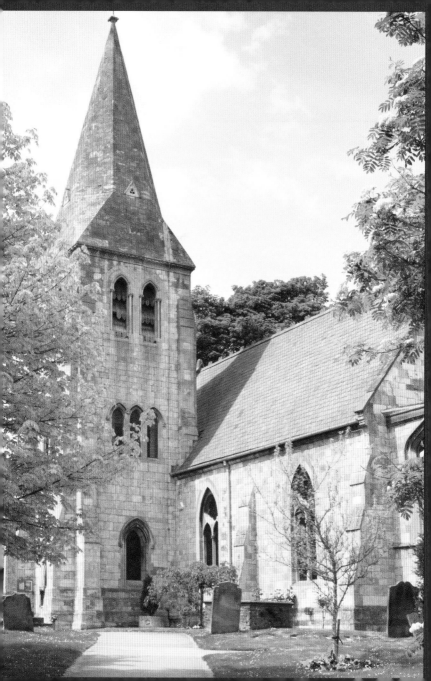

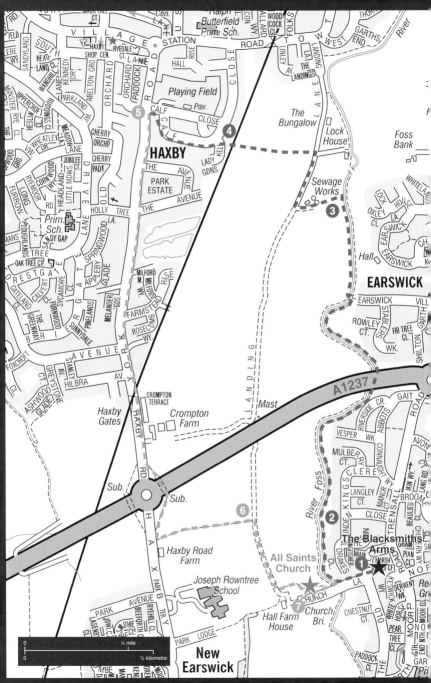

The walk starts from The Blacksmiths Arms ★ on The Old Village road in Huntington. There is a medium-sized car park behind the pub and buses from the city centre stop on nearby North Moor Road. The car park is on the left of the road as you alight the bus, and a passageway from the car park brings you out beside the pub.

1 With your back to The Blacksmiths Arms, turn left and immediately right down a narrow one-track road called Church Lane. Walk along here until just before you reach the bridge, and on your right you will see a wooden entrance to a footpath alongside the river. Go through this entrance and follow the path alongside the river. The path is initially laid with gravel, but later becomes a well trodden dirt path, and you will probably meet several dog walkers and possibly the occasional fishing party along the way.

2 As you walk the path, on your right there will sometimes be houses and sometimes some quite dense wooded areas. The path passes underneath the main York outer ring road and continues out into the countryside. After some distance you will see more houses on the right, and just before you reach them a small foot bridge crosses the river. Take this bridge and cross over to the opposite bank, then turn right and continue along the river in the same direction you have been going.

3 A little while after this, the path turns away from the river at a right angle to the left. Follow this path alongside a field until it meets a gravel road. Turn right and the road immediately becomes paved. Follow it along until you see a fingerpost and a small wooden bridge on your left. Follow this path, it is signposted for Calf Close. This will lead you across the edge of another field and ends in a metal gate to a railway crossing.

4 Go through the gate and ensure the railway is clear in both directions before crossing the tracks and going through the gate on the other side. After passing along a short path, turn right onto the road and then immediately left. This will lead you around Calf Close in a flattened semicircle until you come to a path cutting the corner of a T junction with a children's play park on the opposite side. Turn left here and then left again onto the main York Road.

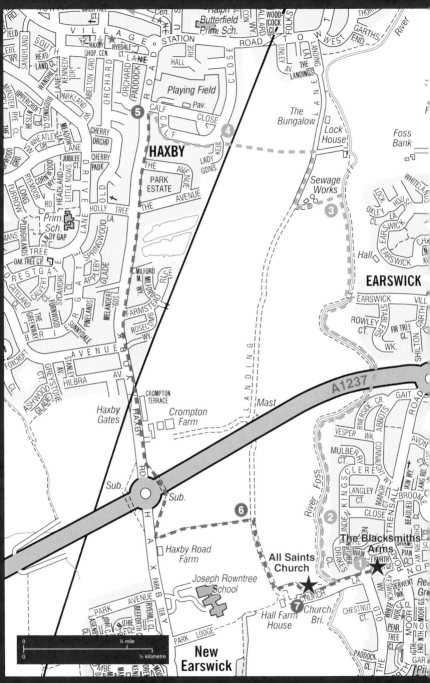

5 Follow this road down for about three-quarters of a mile (1.2 km), crossing the railway again at a level crossing. Shortly after this you reach the York outer ring road again, and the footway passes to the left of this and through an underpass. After you emerge on the other side, a short distance down the road you will come to Tregarth Stables, and just before it you will see a narrow footpath leading away to the left. Follow this path, which runs alongside the Joseph Rowntree School playing fields.

6 Near the end of the path is a metal gate, and shortly afterwards a gravel road crosses. Turn right here and follow this road until just before you reach some farm buildings. Here a path leads away to the left, fingerposted for Church Lane. Follow this and it leads to a wooden gate into the All Saints churchyard ★. Pass around the church, you can go in either direction but passing to the right takes you past the church entrance.

7 Exit the churchyard onto the road and then cross the bridge ahead of you, and you can retrace your steps to your start point, where you have the choice to end your tour in The Blacksmiths Arms itself.

▲Z walk fifteen

Two Norman Churches

Askham Bryan and Askham Richard.

The villages of Askham Bryan and Askham Richard, about 5 miles (8 km) to the southwest of York city centre, were once property of Edwin, Earl of Mercia. After the Norman invasion they were confiscated, and became separate properties. Askham Bryan eventually ended up in the hands of Bryan FitzAlan, a 13th century knight whose name was adopted for the village. Askham Richard is said to be named for a son of King John.

St Nicholas' Church, where we start the walk, is an 11th century Norman church that still retains its original design, with the exception of a 17th century bell tower. Opposite is the village duck pond, where a host of wildlife can often be encountered. As you pass along the main street of Askham Bryan you will pass several interesting buildings, including the Victorian Doctor's House and the village hall, a former Methodist chapel.

Askham Richard is mainly a cluster of quaint cottages, some of which are listed buildings, clustered around the village green. The green itself is well worth seeing, and has a particularly splendid pond at one end. The village also has another Norman church, dating to 1086 but in this case partially rebuilt in 1887.

start / finish	St Nicholas' Church, Main Street, Askham Bryan
nearest postcode	YO23 3QU
distance	2¾ miles / 4.4 km
time	1 hour
terrain	Paved and gravel roads and uneven pathways. Some stiles.

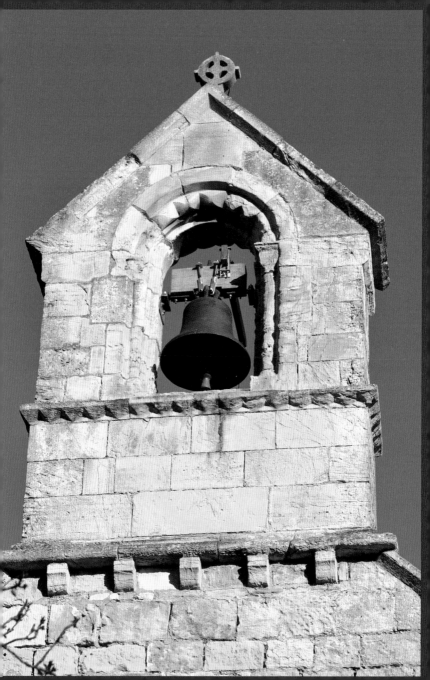

The walk begins at St Nicholas' Church ★ in Askham Bryan. This can be reached by bus from the city centre, setting down at Church Close, a short distance away, and picking up again opposite the village hall. Be aware that this bus only runs three times a day. If you prefer to drive, you can park on-street in front of the church.

1 From the church gate, turn right and walk along the main street of the village. Along the way you will pass the village hall ★ and the Nags Head pub on your left and the Doctor's House ★ on the right. As you come to the end of the village, the pavement ends, so you will have to proceed with care along the narrow road avoiding any traffic, although generally this will be light and not fast moving.

2 You will pass the Poor Clares Monastery ★ on the left, and shortly after this the road turns sharply right, but an unpaved road continues straight ahead, alongside a farmyard. Take this unpaved road and continue along. You will eventually come to a large metal farm gate with a small kissing gate on the left side. Go through this gate and the path leads along the side of a field.

3 At the other end of this field there is a series of two stiles to climb over, and the path then continues along the side of the next field but separated from it by a barbed wire fence. Continue along here until you reach an unpaved road running across the path, on the other side of this is a metal kissing gate leading into a field. Turn left here and use the road.

4 After a short while the road turns 90 degrees to the right with some metal gates ahead of you. Follow this part of the road along and it becomes paved just as you start to see some houses ahead. Continue to follow the road, and at the corner of the buildings, turn right and you will be entering the village green of Askham Richard.

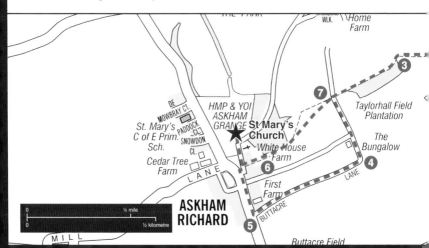

5 You may want to explore the village green a little. When you are finished, continue up the road and as the main road begins to curve to the left, you will notice the footpath divides and goes into a narrower road straight ahead but right of the main one. Take this route, past the Rose & Crown pub and you will see a sign on the wall marked 'To The Church' and a footpath leading to the right marked by a public footpath finger post. We will be taking this path in a moment, but first continue straight ahead and at the end of the road you will find St Mary's Church ★. You may want to explore the grounds of the church, especially the shady cemetery to the rear. When you are done, retrace your steps to the public footpath.

6 Follow this path along as it crosses a stile and then arrives at a metal kissing gate. Go through this gate into the field at the other side, and walk along the left side of the field. As you reach a corner there is a small wooden bridge. Depending on weather conditions there may or may not be water underneath. Cross this bridge and then head diagonally towards the left corner of the rest of the field. You will probably be able to discern the path as being tramped down.

7 At the other side, you will pass through another metal kissing gate. This is the one you saw earlier, and the path you came along from Askham Bryan is directly opposite you. You can now retrace your steps back to your start point.

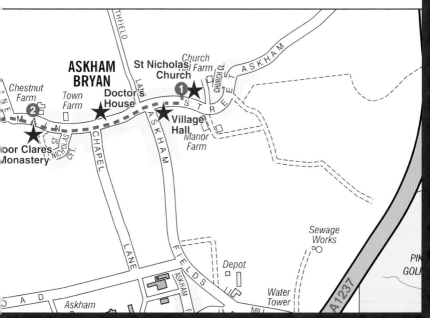

ᴀᴢ walk sixteen

In Bygone Farmers' Footsteps

Stockton on the Forest and Brockfield Hall.

This walk starts from the main street of Stockton on the Forest, a picturesque village clustered around a single road 4 miles (6.4 km) northeast of York. The village is old enough to have been mentioned in the Domesday Book, and stands in the middle of farmland. Many of the paths this walk follows were the main routes used by farmers and farm hands in centuries gone by.

The route of the walk takes you past Brockfield Hall. A late Georgian country house set in beautiful gardens, the house is open to the public only on certain days of the year, with guided tours being conducted by the owners themselves. The house contains the largest collection of works by the Staithes Group of artists, so the tours are a major draw for art enthusiasts.

The village itself also includes Stockton Hall, built in the early 19th century and now a psychiatric hospital, it can be seen from the main road, and the clock tower of the nearby outbuildings overlooks the main street. Further along the street is the similarly named Stockton House, on which a blue plaque announces it as the former home of prominent Methodist philanthropist Thomas Wilkinson and his wife Susannah.

start / finish	The Fox Inn, The Village, Stockton on the Forest
nearest postcode	YO32 9UW
distance	3¼ miles / 5.25 km
time	1 hour 15 minutes
terrain	Some surfaced roads and paths, some gravel roads and dirt paths. Some stiles.

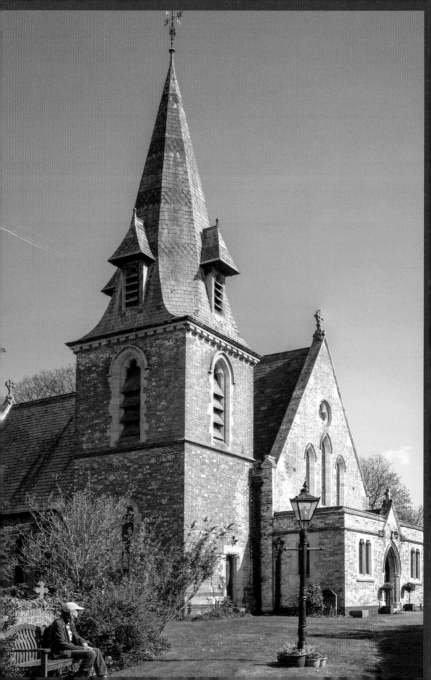

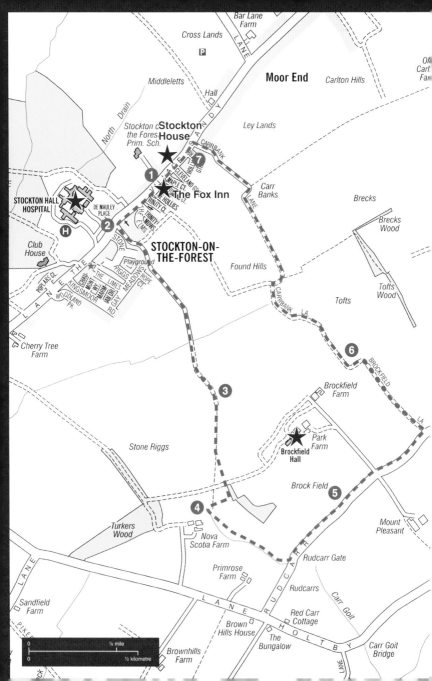

The walk begins from outside The Fox Inn ★ . This can be reached by bus from York, getting off at the stop for Stockton Primary School. Alternatively there is plenty of on-street parking nearby if you are coming by car.

❶ From The Fox, turn left to walk along the main street, just called 'The Village'. Keep an eye on the buildings on the right-hand side of the road, and you will see the clock and bell tower outside Stockton Hall ★ .

❷ Just before you pass this tower, you will see two gravel roads next to each other on your left, with two signs reading 'Stockton Lane' and 'Laurel House'. Take the second of these two roads, it is called Beanland Lane. The gravel lane will gradually get narrower and then become a dirt path through grassland.

❸ Keep following this path. There are finger posts and yellow route indicators along the way indicating that it is a public footpath, so you shouldn't lose the way. Shortly after crossing through the centre of a large wheatfield, you will come to a right-angle turn, with a finger post indicating Rudcarr Lane in a quarter of a mile. Turn and follow this, and at the end of this field you will see a stile on your left.

❹ Cross this stile and cross the next field at a diagonal. You should see the path in the grass, and at the opposite side the field narrows and another stile takes you out onto a surfaced road.

Turn left and follow this road, being careful of traffic as it has no kerb but does have grass verges that you can use to avoid any cars that come along.

❺ As you walk along this road, you will be able to see Brockfield Hall ★ through the trees on your left. Keep going along this road, passing the driveway that leads to Brockfield Hall and Brockfield Farm, and shortly after there is a track on the left with a metal barrier and a finger post indicating that it is a public bridleway. Turn down here, and as you walk you will get good views of Brockfield Farm and the wall of the Brockfield Hall gardens.

❻ As you draw level with Brockfield Farm, the path turns sharp left and then sharp right. Keep following the path, at times it becomes a little overgrown but is still visible. A short distance further on there is another sharp right and then left turn, and then another sharp right. Just after this you will see a fingerpost indicating that the path can go one of two ways. Follow the one marked 'Stockton on the Forest' and this will lead you back to the main road opposite a sign indicating that this part of the road is called Sandy Lane.

❼ Turn left here and follow the main road, passing Stockton House ★ and some other nice Victorian houses on the right. Eventually this will bring you back to The Fox, where you may wish to enjoy some refreshments.

ᴀᴢ walk seventeen

Medieval and Modern

Skelton and Rawcliffe Landing.

The village of Skelton lies just outside the York outer ring road on the main A19 road to Thirsk. Although much of what can be seen from the road looks modern, this walk will take you through the older part of the village, past many of the houses that hark back to when this was an agricultural village supplying food for the city, several of which are listed buildings.

The village has a number of open spaces, including a pond that we will walk past. The Church of St Giles lies at the heart of the community and dates back to 1247, having been restored but largely unchanged in the years since. It is said to be one of the most complete early English churches remaining in the country. The stone it was built with may have been donated by Archbishop Walter de Grey from material left over after building the south transept of York Minster.

After a wander around the village, we then cross the A19 for a pleasant walk leading past the River Ouse in an area popular for canoeing and river swimming. The walk starts and ends at the Fairfield Manor Hotel, now owned by a hotel chain but built around an early Georgian mansion standing in six acres of grounds that was home to several notable local families in the 18th and 19th centuries.

start / finish	Fairfield Manor Hotel, Shipton Road, Skelton
nearest postcode	YO30 1XW
distance	2¼ miles / 3.75 km
time	45 minutes
terrain	Mostly roads and paved pathways.

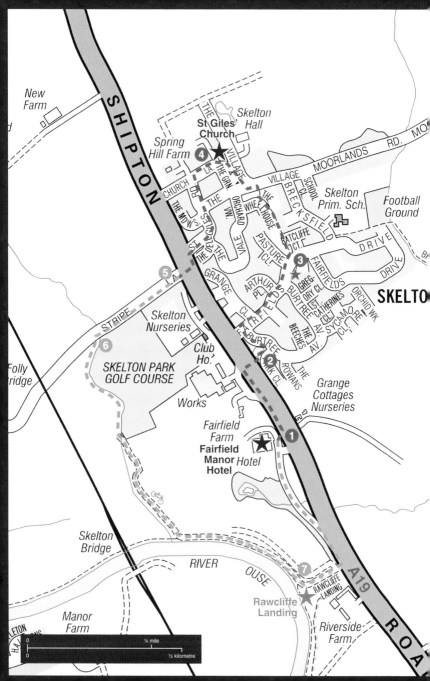

The walk starts from the Fairfield Manor Hotel ★ . Several buses from the city stop right outside, and there is a large layby next to it with plenty of space to park a car.

1 From in front of the hotel, go to your left and walk up the road until just before the next turning on the left. Cross the main A19 road here, using the defined crossing and the island in the middle.

2 At the other side, there is a gap in the hedge directly ahead of you, go through this and you are next to Skelton village pond. Follow the path alongside the pond, and go left at the road to continue following it round. When the road turns away from the pond, go this way to reach a T junction. Turn right onto Fairfields Drive and follow this along. Cross to the opposite side when it is safe.

3 Just past a turning on the left for Pasture Close, you will see a paved footpath also on the left. Turn onto this and follow it up through some parkland. When you reach a road again, cross and turn left, then immediately right into the village green. There is a turning on the left, and then a fork in the road. Take the left fork and this will lead you up past St Giles' Church ★ . The gate is towards the end of this road on the right if you want to explore the church itself.

4 Otherwise turn right at the end of this short road, and then almost immediately left into Church Lane. Take the next left into St Giles Road, and follow this down until it joins a road curving in from the left. Keep going on this road as it curves round to the right and then returns to the main A19 road. Turn left and pass the bus stop to where there is a traffic island that will allow you to cross the road safely.

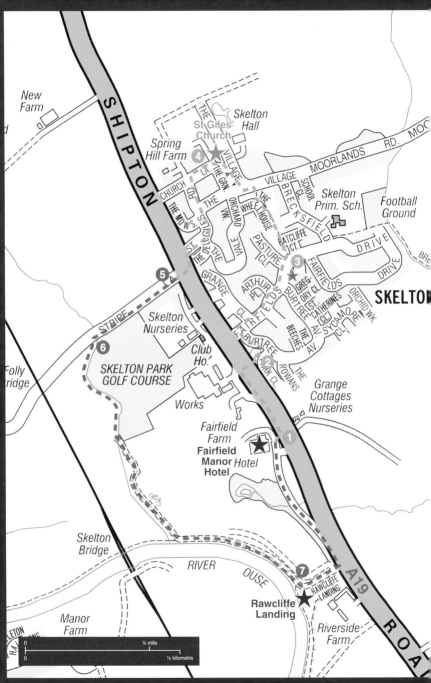

5 As you cross the road, there is a narrow lane leading away from the A19 almost directly opposite and signposted for Overton. Follow this road, being careful of traffic. After a while the road dips down a slope at the bottom of which you will see a footpath on the left signposted for York. There is a model of a cyclist and a dog on top of the signpost.

6 Turn and follow this path, it winds its way into some woods, crossing a bridge that has been mocked up to look like a miniature Forth Rail Bridge. Keep following this path through the woods, eventually it finds its way to the bank of the Ouse. Follow the path to the left, alongside the river. Just before the path veers left away from the river at Rawcliffe Landing ★, you may notice a small metal gate on your right. Through here is a grassy bank sloping down to the river used often by canoeists and river swimmers to access the river.

7 However, we are not going through the gate, instead continue along the path as it passes alongside a large metal gate and becomes a road again. Follow this road, noting on your right there is a large marker post for York taking the form of a globe with models of the city's attractions attached. Once you reach the A19 road, turn left and follow the footpath until you reach a large layby separated from the road on the left. Use this layby to continue along the road, and you will return to your starting point.

ᴀᴢ walk eighteen

Wildlife and Ancient Woodland

Dunnington village, Hassacarr Nature Reserve
and Hagg Wood.

This walk starts in the village of Dunnington, about 5 miles (8 km) east of
York city centre. There has been a settlement here since Anglo-Saxon times.
St Nicholas' Church has a 15th century Norman-style clock tower and some
of the internal structure dates to the 11th century.

The route of the tour runs through Hassacarr Nature Reserve, a small
nationally recognized conservation area which occupies part of the land of
the former Derwent Valley Light Railway. Some of this nature reserve can
be visited, other parts are restricted due to the delicate nature of the animal
habitats there.

We also walk through Hagg Wood, an area of ancient woodland mentioned
in the Domesday Book. While this walk passes straight through the wood,
there are plenty of side paths to explore, and the wood is home to countless
species of birds and insects, as well as foxes and roe deer. If in season, there
are wonderful displays of foxgloves along the way.

start / finish	St Nicholas' Church, Church Street, Dunnington
nearest postcode	YO19 5PW
distance	4¾ miles / 7.8 km
time	2 hours
terrain	Surfaced roads and paths, gravelled road, some woodland paths.

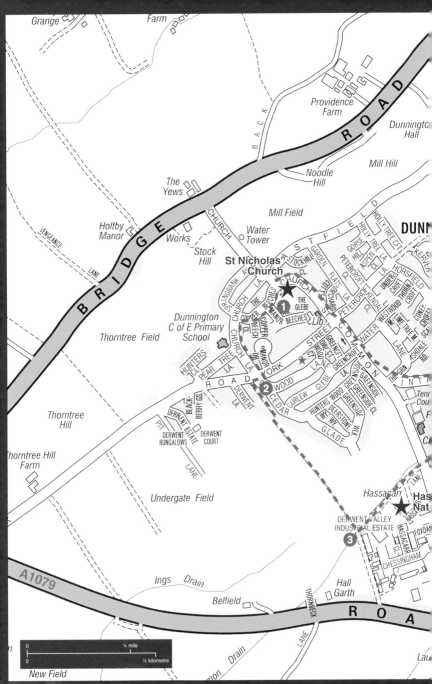

We start at St Nicholas' Church ★.
Buses from York stop just outside, and
there is plenty of on-street parking
nearby.

1 Turn left from the church entrance,
leaving Church Street through a short
cut into The Copper Beeches, and
follow this road along to the end. At the
crossroads, turn left into Church Lane.
Where the road turns right to become
Pear Tree Lane, follow Church Lane
which continues as a one-track lane
leading off to the left.

2 At the crossroads with York Road,
cross carefully to the other side and
turn right. In just a few yards there is
a narrow path leading off to the left
between house numbers 67 and 69.
Turn into this path and follow it until it
turns right and leads you to the edge
of a field. Turn left and follow the path
along the edge of this field and shortly
afterwards the path veers diagonally to
the right. Follow this, into another field
where, again, you follow the edge of
the field.

3 Shortly afterwards you reach a
large warehouse, and just before this a
track leads off to the left. Follow this to
a set of gates after which it becomes
a gravel road, At this point you are in
the Hassacarr Nature Reserve ★, and
there is shortly a path off to the right
leading to a picturesque pond if you
want to explore the area. Otherwise,
continue along this road until you reach
the main road, then carefully cross
and take the next gravel road on the
opposite side.

4 Just before you arrive at a
whitewashed cottage, there is a kissing
gate on your right, waymarked with a
yellow arrow. Go through this gate and
diagonally across the field on the other
side. After going through a second
gate and again diagonally across
the next field, you arrive at another
waymarked spot where a small footpath
heading right is slightly separated from
the fields. Follow this as it passes round
a small pond, until you arrive at a one-
track lane.

5 Turn left onto this lane, past Primrose Farm until you reach a set of gates and a finger post reading 'Public Footpath, Hagg Wood'. Turn left to follow this path, and continue to follow as it turns right. Follow this path as it enters Hagg Wood ★ , and continue on this path through the wood. If you want to explore the rest of the wood, when you have finished look for waymarkers that point to the North Entrance and this will get you back on the correct route.

6 Leaving the wood, you will arrive at another waymarker post. Turn left and follow this path along the edge of the field until it turns right across the field. At this point there is also a lane on the left, with another waymarker post and a blue sign indicating that it is part of the Way of the Roses cycle route. Turn left and follow this path all the way back to Dunnington. Along the way it passes through another gate, and shortly afterwards becomes the gravel road Intake Lane.

7 Towards the end of the road you pass a play park and the road curves right. As it approaches the end it joins another road coming in from the right just before a T junction. Across from here there is a grass area with a footpath on the right in front of a set of cottages. Take this footpath and continue until it joins the main road again. Shortly after this you will arrive at the main junction of the village with a small stone monument in the centre. Continue straight ahead here and up the hill and it will bring you back to your start point.

ᴀᴢ walk nineteen
Small Village with a Big History
Strensall village and common.

Strensall is a historic village lying on the River Foss, 6 miles (9.6 km) north of York. The village has existed for at least a thousand years, being mentioned in the Domesday Book and earlier referenced by the Venerable Bede. Much of its importance in years gone by were due to the river being used to transport goods towards Sheriff Hutton. Later it became an important stop on the York to Scarborough railway line. The railway station is now closed and the river is no longer navigable, but the village retains its share of interest.

South of the village is Strensall Common. Originally Lords Moor Farm, part of the common was purchased by the government to become a military training ground, and remains as such today. Access to the common itself is therefore dependent on whether exercises are taking place. The eastern end of the common is a nature reserve with heathland and woodland, and an abundance of bird and plant species as well as lizards and hares.

The village used to lie in the heart of the Forest of Galtres, the ancient hunting ground of the Norman kings, which lay to the north of 'Old Humpy', the oldest surviving brick-built bridge over the Foss. As you walk along the river, look out for interesting wildlife, including herons and buzzards.

start / finish	Strensall Explore Library, The Village, Strensall
nearest postcode	YO32 5XS
distance	4½ miles / 7 km
time	1 hour 45 minutes
terrain	Mixture of surfaced and dirt paths and roads. One stile.

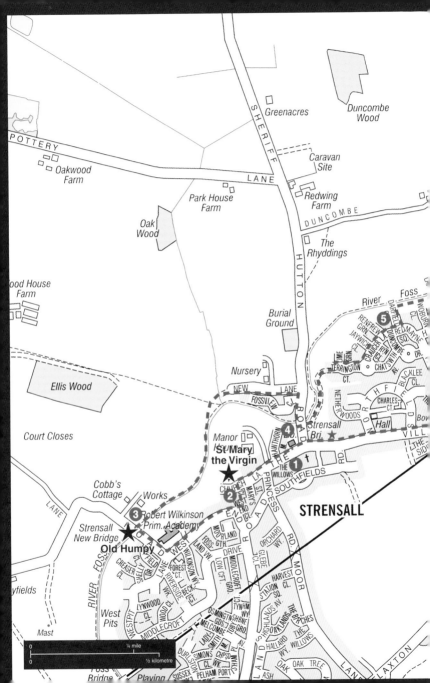

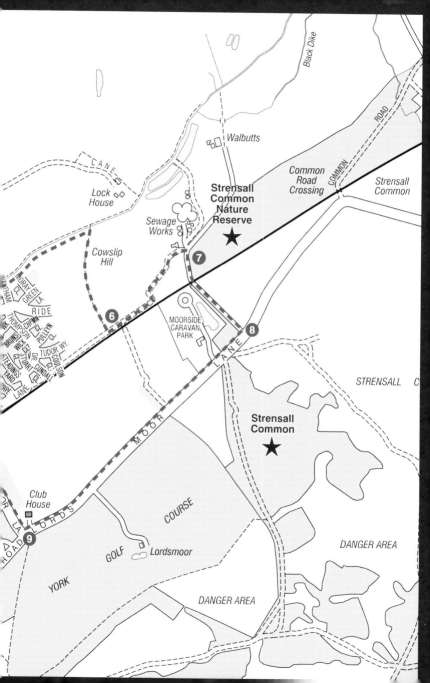

Black Dike

Walbutts

COMMON ROAD

**Strensall
Common
Nature
Reserve**

Common
Road
Crossing

Strensall
Common

★

Lock
House

LANE

Sewage
Works

Cowslip
Hill

GREEN LA.
WALTHAM
MORAY CL.
THOMP-CHPMN
WICK CL.
BRUNS
STEADNESS YARD
DR. STUART CL.
TUDOR WY.
COULSON
CUNDA
PULLEIN CL.

RIDE

6

7

MOORSIDE
CARAVAN
PARK

8

LANE

STRENSALL   C

MOOR

**Strensall
Common**

★

Club
House

LORDS

COURSE

DANGER AREA

9

ROAD LA.

GOLF

Lordsmoor

YORK

DANGER AREA

DANGER AREA

The walk begins in front of the Explore Library, next door to the Ship Inn. There is a set down from the bus from York here, or on-street parking in the nearby streets.

1 From in front of the library, go right and follow the main road a short distance until it turns sharply left. Instead of following the road, go straight ahead into Church Lane, until you reach the parish church of St Mary the Virgin ★.

2 Opposite the church is a wide footpath with metal barriers. At the other end, passing through more metal barriers, turn right and head straight on to West End Close. Continue along this road until a grassy area on the right precedes a turning to the right onto Haxby Moor Road. Follow this road along to the 'Old Humpy' bridge ★ and cross this, being careful as it is narrow with no footpath and carries traffic.

3 Immediately across the bridge, some wooden steps to the right, signposted for Sheriff Hutton Road, take you down to the riverbank, where a well-worn dirt path leads you alongside the river. Further along the path divides in two, one side to the left

going through a wooden gate. You can take either path, the riverside one leads to a clearer path around the outside of a housing development, or the left-hand path leads to a gravel lane at the end of which you will need to turn right to arrive at the same point.

4 You are now at the John Carr Bridge, another narrow bridge but this one has a newer footbridge to the right-hand side. Cross this and then cross the road to where a wooden gateway leads you to a surfaced footpath. Follow this footpath, initially alongside the river and then as it veers away. It eventually brings you to Terrington Court. Follow this road along to a small roundabout and take the left-hand turning into Chaucer Lane.

5 Take the third turning on the left along here, into Darfield Close, and you will see some stone bollards ahead with a path leading back to the riverside. Take this path, then turn right and follow the dirt path along the bank of the river. Continue until the path veers at a right angle away from the river to the right. Follow this, and shortly afterwards is a metal gate into a field. Go through, and follow along the right-hand side of the field to another metal gate that leads you out onto a gravel lane.

6 Go straight ahead along this lane until you reach a T junction with a surfaced road. Turn left and follow this road, initially alongside the railway and then as it turns first left then right away from it. Keep going and on the right you will see a green and yellow waymarker next to a sign for Strensall Common Nature Reserve ★ . A path leads through the woods here away to your right, follow this until you reach another path with a wooden gate opposite you. Turn right here and continue to follow the path.

7 This leads you back to the railway line which you will have to cross carefully making sure no trains are coming. There is a set of steps at one side of the line and a wooden stile at the other side which you will need to cross. Then keep going straight on through the woods until you reach the main road.

8 Turn right and follow the road along. There is no footpath so you will need to use the grass verge to avoid any traffic. To your left as you walk along here initially you will be passing military training grounds, and later the York Golf Club. On the way along you will need to pass through a wooden gate to the right of a cattle grid.

9 Just after you pass the entry sign for Strensall on your left, there is a turning on the right next to the York Golf Club clubhouse. Take this turning and follow this road along, crossing from the right to left pavement half way along. Shortly after this, cross the level crossing and the road then turns sharply to the left. Continue along this road and you will return to your start point, where you can catch the bus back to York or reward yourself with a stop at the Ship Inn.

ᴀᴢ walk twenty

Country Estate Circuit

Beningbrough Hall and Newton-on-Ouse.

Newton-on-Ouse is a small village of not much more than 500 inhabitants around 10 miles (16 km) northwest of York. The village has existed at least since Saxon times, the River Kyle meeting the Ouse at this point making it a perfect spot for a settlement. The church of All Saints in the village is mostly Victorian in construction, but its tower and spire are around 900 years old.

This walk is best combined with a visit to Beningbrough Hall, which lies just outside the village. The walk will take you around the outside of the grounds of the hall, with great views of this magnificent Georgian mansion built in 1716 as a home for John Bourchier III, a wealthy York landowner and later High Sheriff of Yorkshire. Sitting on an estate of 300 acres (1.2 square kilometres), it is surrounded by 8 acres of formal gardens which can be explored during a visit.

The parkland of the hall is free to visit, and much of this walk skirts the edges of it. The first half runs along the bank of the River Ouse, and along the way passes a 19th century castellated water tower, and later a small beach area popular with locals on sunny summer days.

start / finish	Newton-on-Ouse village green
nearest postcode	YO30 2DE
distance	3½ miles / 5.75 km
time	1 hour 15 minutes
terrain	Mostly pathways of mixed terrain, some paved road.

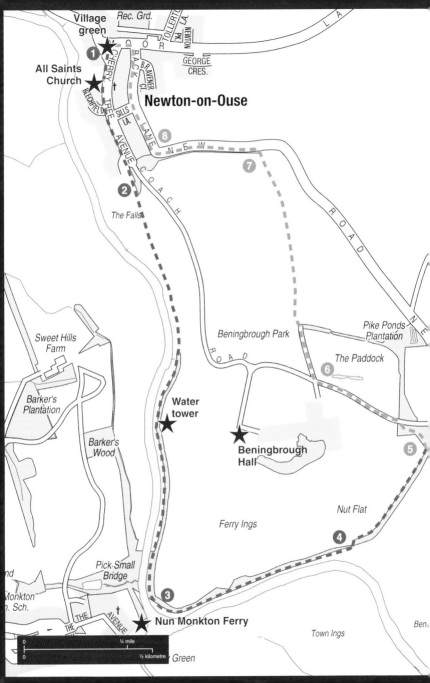

This walk starts from the village green ★ of Newton-on-Ouse. The village is quite out of the way, and can be reached by bus from York, but be warned there are only four buses a day, so be careful with timings. This walk is better reached by car, following signposts for Newton-on-Ouse from the main A19 York to Thirsk road. Parking in the village is on the roadside.

➊ From the village green take Cherry Tree Avenue leading south. You will recognize it because the church of All Saints ★ is on the right of the road. Continue down the road until you reach the lodge and gates of Beningbrough Hall, where a small one-track road runs diagonally away to the right, signposted as a public footpath. Follow this road to the end, past some houses on your right and into a field.

➋ Follow along the left side of this field, until you see the main riverside footpath on a raised embankment. Join this path, heading to your left and into some trees that line the riverbank. There is a second path further down next to the river that you may use if you wish, but you will need to return to the main path before you reach the tall water tower ★. You will encounter this tower along the path, and you need to pass through the wooden gate on the right and then continue along the path.

➌ As the river turns sharply to the left, there is a small beach area on the bend. Across on the other bank you will see the wooden docks for the Nun Monkton Ferry ★. This only runs on Saturdays and Sundays in summer, but makes a pleasant addition to the walk if it is operating. Otherwise continue along the path as it follows the river and as you walk this stretch you will get some wonderful views of the rear of Beningbrough Hall ★ through the trees on your left.

➍ Continuing on this path, just before the river bends away to the right, you will pass through a wooden entryway, and shortly afterwards arrive at two wooden gates next to each other. The right-hand gate leads to a narrow path along the side of a field. You need to take the left-hand gate however, which runs into some woods and the path through them parallels that first path.

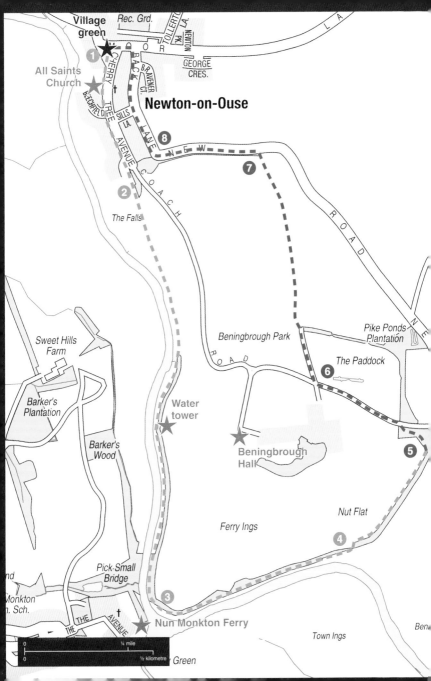

Village green

Rec. Grd.

All Saints Church

Newton-on-Ouse

GEORGE CRES.

❶

❷

❸

❹

❺

❻

❼

❽

The Falls

Sweet Hills Farm

Barker's Plantation

Barker's Wood

Beningbrough Park

Pike Ponds Plantation

The Paddock

Water tower

Beningbrough Hall

Nut Flat

Pick·Small Bridge

Monkton n. Sch.

Nun Monkton Ferry

Ferry Ings

Town Ings

Green

¼ mile

½ kilometre

5 Pass through two more wooden gates and follow the path as it turns away to the left. Shortly after this, you will arrive at a metal fence with a gate and a paved road on the other side. Go through this gate and turn left. This road will lead you into the grounds of Beningbrough Hall, and you will start to see farm buildings on your left.

6 You will arrive at a crossroads, with a sign advertising Home Farm Café on your left. You need to take the road to the right. It has wooden gates that may be closed, but on the right is a pedestrian access gate with a sign reading 'Larch Walk'. Follow this along and at the end you will see two large metal gates with a small wooden one in between. Go through the wooden gate and follow the path through a small enclosure and out of the other side. Keep following this path. After a while there is a large wooden frame alongside the path. If you turn round you will see that this marks the spot with the best possible view of Beningbrough Hall.

7 Shortly afterwards you will reach a wooden gate with a surfaced road on the other side. A path leads away through the woods on your left. At this point you can either follow this path, or pass through the gate and turn left. Either way will take you to the same place.

8 If you use the path, this will emerge next to the sign announcing you are once again entering Newton-on-Ouse. The road turns sharply right at this point. Follow this road all the way back into the village. You might want to note a memorial on the right of the road to the crew of a Halifax Bomber which crashed near this spot in 1944. When you reach the top of this road, turn left and you will return to your start point.